Warman's®
COMPANION

McCOY
POTTERY

Mark F. Moran

©2006 Krause Publications

Published by

700 East State Street • Iola, WI 54990-0001
715-445-2214 • 888-457-2873

Our toll-free number to place an order or obtain
a free catalog is (800) 258-0929.

Library of Congress Catalog Number: 2005935073
ISBN 13-digit: 978-0-89689-306-1
ISBN 10-digit: 0-89689-306-5

Designed by Marilyn McGrane and Kay Sanders
Edited by Dennis Thornton

Printed in China

Table of Contents

A Family Tradition

To Begin With ...

This book does not contain every single piece of Mc-Coy pottery. No book does, and perhaps no single book could. The variety and volume of wares produced by the several incarnations of McCoy potteries during more than 14 decades are stagger-ing, and previously unknown or experi-mental pieces are still being found today. But thanks to a gen-erous and devoted group of collectors willing to share their time and treasures, this volume presents a detailed view of the products of an American institution.

The first McCoy with clay under his fingernails was W. Nelson McCoy. With his uncle, W.F. McCoy, he founded a pottery works in Putnam, Ohio, in 1848, making stoneware crocks and jugs.

That same year, W. Nelson's son, James W., was born in Zanesville, Ohio. James established the J.W. McCoy Pottery Co. in Roseville, Ohio, in the fall of 1899. The J.W. McCoy plant was destroyed by fire in 1903, and was rebuilt two years later.

It was at this time that the first examples of Loy-Nel-Art wares were produced. The line's distinc-tive title came from the names of James McCoy's three sons, Lloyd, Nelson, and Arthur. Like other "standard" glazed pieces produced at this time by several Ohio potteries, Loy-Nel-Art has a glossy finish on a dark brown-black body, but Loy-Nel-Art featured a splash of green color on the front, and a burnt-orange splash on the back.

George Brush became general manager of J.W. McCoy Pottery Co. in 1909. The company became Brush-McCoy Pottery Co. in 1911, and in 1925 the name was shortened to Brush Pottery Co. This firm remained in business until 1982.

Separately, in 1910, Nelson McCoy Sr. founded the Nelson McCoy Sanitary and Stoneware Co., also in Roseville. By the early 1930s, production had shift-ed from utilitarian wares to art pottery, and the com-pany name was changed to Nelson McCoy Pottery.

Designer Sydney Cope was hired in 1934, and was joined by his son, Leslie, in 1936. The Copes' influence on McCoy wares continued until Syd-ney's death in 1966. That same year, Leslie opened a gallery devoted to his family's design heritage and featuring his own original art.

Nelson McCoy Sr. died in 1945, and was suc-ceeded as company president by his nephew, Nel-son McCoy Melick.

A fire destroyed the plant in 1950, but company officials—including Nelson McCoy Jr., then 29—decided to rebuild, and the new Nelson McCoy Pottery Co. was up and running in just six months.

Nelson Melick died in 1954. Nelson Jr. became company president, and oversaw the company's continued growth. In 1967, the operation was sold to entrepreneur David Chase. At this time, the words "Mt. Clemens Pottery" were added to the company marks. In 1974, Chase sold the company to Lancaster Colony Corp., and the company marks included a stylized "LCC" logo. Nelson Jr. and his wife, Billie, who had served as a products supervisor, left the company in 1981.

In 1985, the company was sold again, this time to Designer Accents. The McCoy pottery factory closed in 1990.

Words of Thanks

This book would not have been possible without the help and good wishes of the following:

• Carol Seaman and Dan Eggert of Brecksville, Ohio. Carol publishes the NM Xpress newsletter, and can be reached at http://www.members.aol.com/nmxpress/

• John and Polly Sweetman of Townsend, Del., whose Web site is http://www.mccoylovers.com/mcgoldtrim/

  • Kathleen Moloney of New York, N.Y.
  • Pat and Royal Ritchey of Cullman, Ala.
  • Basil and Dianna Atkins, Ohio
  • Janel Schultz of Winona, Minn.
  • Rose Kowles of Winona, Minn.

From Top: The Nelson McCoy Pottery Co. in Roseville, Ohio, is shown in a vintage photo, probably from the 1930s.
A fire destroyed the McCoy factory in 1950, but the plant was rebuilt and was operating again in six months.
Workers inspect the burned-out remains of the McCoy pottery factory in 1950.
The new Nelson McCoy Pottery Co. plant opened after the 1950 fire and operated under various owners until it closed in 1990.

Cookie Jars

Cookie jars represent one of most popular categories for McCoy collectors. Even the most enthusiastic collectors admit that the McCoy lid designs and configurations contribute to the dings and cracks common on these pieces, so condition is an important consideration. Many jars also have cold-paint decoration (done by hand on top of the glazed surfaces) and this paint is easily worn. Examples with good paint bring a premium price. This category has also been plagued by fakes. Knowing the correct dimensions of the real jars is vital for beginning collectors.

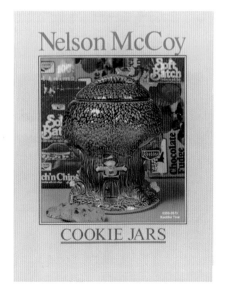

Hand Crafted Cookie Jars

22-0156-73

22-0201-73

WOODSY OWL

22-0202-11

Assortment 22-0173-55

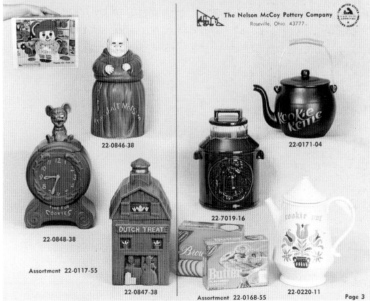

The Nelson McCoy Pottery Company
Roseville, Ohio 43777

22-0846-38

22-0171-04

22-0848-38

DUTCH TREAT

22-7019-16

Assortment 22-0117-55

22-0847-38

22-0220-11

Assortment 22-0168-55

Page 3

Opposite: A flyer promoted the Keebler Treehouse cookie jar.
Above: Several cookie jars, including Woodsy Owl, a monk,
and a Kookie Kettle, were featured in the 1973 McCoy catalog.

Cookies

Right: Apollo jar with original paper flag and label, 1970-71, McCoy mark.   **$350-$400**

Below: Two Apple jars. Red example is late 1950s, McCoy USA mark, and same form as Blushing Apple jars, but is cold painted with gold finial.   **$75-$85**
White Apple jar, nicknamed "The Tooth," has a leaf lid found on other fruit-form jars, early 1970s, McCoy USA mark.   **$50-$60**

Two variations of Apple jars: above, as it came from the factory without leaf knob; at right, flat-leaf apple with strong burgundy and yellow glaze.

Asparagus jar, 1970s.   **$75-$85**

Astronaut jar, 1960s, USA mark. (Rarely in dark blue.)   **$350-$400**

Cookies

Hand-painted ball jar with slanted knob (also comes with rectangular knob), stoneware, late 1930s to early 1950s, unmarked. (This shape was reissued in the mid-1960s.) **$45-$55** (depending on paint condition)

Ball jar in cobalt blue, 1940s, unmarked, 6 1/2" tall. **$90-$110**

Two versions of the Banana jar, 1948, McCoy mark. Left is the more typical glaze. Often found with damage to lid points. **$200-$250** (depending on color)

Baseball Boy and Football Boy jars, late 1970s to early '80s, McCoy USA mark. Beware of reproductions. **$175-$225 each** (with the Baseball Boy in the higher range)

Barn jar with cow in door, 1960s, McCoy USA mark, lid was easily damaged.
$350-$400

Two Basket-weave jars, late 1950s, McCoy USA mark, one topped with apples, the other with pears. The word "Cookies" was cold-painted and is often worn; often found with damage to fruit.
$100-$125 each

Two Basket-weave jars, late 1950s, McCoy USA mark, one topped with pine cones, the other with a puppy. The word "Cookies" was cold-painted and is often worn; often found with damage to lids.
$100-$125 each

Above: Two versions of the Bear with Cookie in Vest. At left is an unusual color combination with cold-painted lid. **$350-$450**

Right: Jar has cold-paint trim on white. (Originally from the mid-1940s, this jar was also made in the 1950s with the word "Cookies" between the bear's feet.) **$90-$110**

Below: Reproduction Bear with Cookie in Vest, left, next to the original. New jar is shorter and much lighter than original and was not made by McCoy, despite having an impressed McCoy mark on the base.

Big Orange jar, early 1970s, McCoy USA mark, cold-painted stem and leaves. **$90-$110**

Two Blushing Apple jars, 1950s and '60s, McCoy USA mark. Example at left has leaf finial in wrong position. (Rarely found with saw-tooth leaf on lid.) Typically about **$75** With misplaced finial **$100**

Left: Bobby Baker jar, 1970s, McCoy USA mark, also comes in lower flat hat. **$50-$60** Right: Betsy Baker, 1970s, McCoy USA mark, also comes in ruffled hat. **$175-$225** With rare rounded hat with button top, called "Betty Baker." **$300**

Above left: Bubbles the Pig jar/bank with original box, late 1970s, McCoy USA mark; Teddy and Friend in factory glazes with original box; Chilly Willy in factory glazes with original box.

$75-$100 each

Below left: Reproduction Cauliflower Mammy jar. **$25-$30**

Below right: Real Cauliflower Mammy jar with expected worn cold paint. (Prices for this jar once hovered around $1,000, but the reproductions have driven values down.) **$500-$600**

Chairman of the Board in maroon pants (he also comes with brown pants), 1985, marked 162-USA.
$400-$500

The following is from NM Xpress (http://www.members.aol.com/nmxpress/), Carol Seaman and Dan Eggert, Brecksville, Ohio:

Chairman of the Board: The Chairman of the Board jar was produced in 1985. It was designed during the brief time that Lancaster Colony owned McCoy. It came in two versions: maroon and brown pants. Both the original and reproduction are marked 162-USA. The original Chairman stands 10 5/8" tall and the reproduction is 9 3/4" tall. Once again, height can help you determine the authenticity of this cookie jar.

Chef, 1960s, McCoy USA mark. (Also found with blue face and other scarf colors.) Beware of reproductions shorter than 11". **$175-$200**

Chilly Willy holiday variation, hand-painted at home in Christmas colors by a McCoy employee, late 1980s, USA mark.
Because of paint **$175-$225**
Normally **$75-$100**

Chipmunk jar, early 1960s, McCoy USA mark. (This is easily distinguished from the rare and expensive Squirrel jar—sometimes called Fox Squirrel—which has a much larger tail and is valued at about $4,000.) **$100-$125**

Circus Horse with Monkey jar, 1961, Mc-Coy USA mark, cold-painted details, easily damaged. **$150-$200**

Two versions of Clown in a Barrel jar, mid-1950s, McCoy USA mark, cold-painted details.
$100-$125

Two versions of Clown in a Barrel, mid-1950s, McCoy USA mark, cold-painted details. **$100-$125**

Two versions of Clown in a Barrel, mid-1950s, McCoy USA mark, cold-painted details on all white example, all green example is rare. **$400-$500 each**

Above: Cookie Box (also called the Jewel Box), 1963, USA mark. **$150-$175**

Left: Clyde the Dog jar, mid-1970s, McCoy USA LCC mark, cold-painted details. **$250-$300**

Left: Cookie Bank (modeled on the actual Main Street bank building in Roseville, Ohio), with money slot on reverse, 1960s, McCoy Bank mark. Right: Cookie Cabin, 1950s, unmarked, with cold-painted details. **$90-$110 each**

Cookie Boy jar in turquoise with crisp mold detail, early 1940s, McCoy mark. (Rarely found bare headed.)
$300-$350

Cookie Boy jars in yellow and white, early 1940s, McCoy mark.
$200-$225 each

Two cookie jars in gold trim, late 1940s to '50s. Sack of Cookies has McCoy USA mark, other jar unmarked. **$40-$50 each**

Cookie Special jar, early 1960s, McCoy USA mark, cold-painted details.   **$125-$175**

Engine jar, early 1960s, McCoy USA mark, cold-painted details.
   $125-$175 each
Other color combinations found on engine.

Two other color combinations for Engine jar. **$250-$300 each**

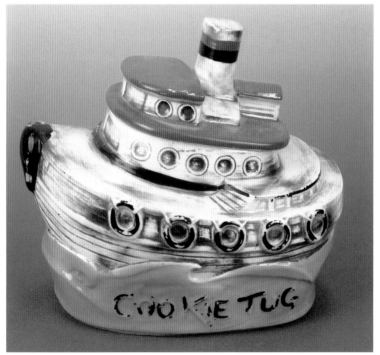

Cookie Tug jar with cold-paint decoration, 1950s, McCoy USA mark.
$8,000-$10,000

Left: Cookie Wagon (also called the "Conestoga Wagon"), 1960s, McCoy USA mark, with glaze and cold paint. **$75-$90**

Right: Cookie House, late 1950s, McCoy USA mark, with split roof lid, easily damaged, with glaze and cold paint. **$125-$140**

Cork crock jar, 1975, McCoy USA mark, can be hard to find complete because lid often broke. **$90-$110**

Down on the Farm Cow, early 1990s, Designer Accents mark. **$90-$110** (Not to be confused with the rare Reclining Cow—also known as "Cookies and Milk Cow"—which sold at auction for $10,000.)

Left: Reproduction Davy Crockett jar.
Right: Original Crockett jar, late 1950s, USA mark, all decoration under glaze. (Prices for this jar once hovered around $700, but the reproductions have driven values down.) **$450-$550**

The following is from NM Xpress (http://www.members.aol.com/nmxpress/), Carol Seaman and Dan Eggert, Brecksville, Ohio:

Davy Crockett: Made by McCoy in 1957, the original Davy jar is 10 1/4" tall and is marked USA on the bottom. In 1994, reproductions of Davy Crockett surfaced, believed to have their origin in Ohio. The reproductions are marked the same (USA) but they don't measure up. The reproduction is barely 9 1/2" tall, making height a good way to tell whether or not it is "the real McCoy!"

Two versions of Dog-house with Bird jar, left being more common, 1980s, later reissued by Lancaster Colony.
$175-$200
(The same dog and bird forms on the front of the jar were found on a rare pair of bookends—possibly for sales samples—that sold at auction for $4,000.)

Two versions of the Drum jar, 1960, McCoy USA mark, all cold-painted so examples may be found nearly white. Red, white, and blue is more common than brown and yellow.
$90-$110 each

Duck on Basket-weave, 1950s, McCoy USA mark, cold-painted details.
$90-$110

Two versions of the Elephant jar, both with cold-painted details. Example at left is called "split trunk" and is harder to find, 1940s, unmarked.
$275-$300
Example at right has complete trunk as part of lid, 1950s, unmarked.
$150-$175

Fireplace lamp and cookie jar made from the same mold, late 1960s, USA mark.
Lamp (rare)   **$125-$150**
Jar   **$75-$100**

Forbidden Fruit jar, late 1960s, McCoy USA mark, with cold paint on the lid.
$90-$110

Flat-leaf Apple cookie jar, glossy maroon, 1930s. **$125-$150**

Flowerpot jar, 1960s, flower forms vary and can be replaced. **$175-$225**

Freddie the Gleep, mid-1970s, cold-paint details (also available in lime green), has been reproduced slightly smaller. **$350-$400**

Friendship 7 jar, 1960s, unmarked, cold-paint details. **$100-$125**

Frontier Family jar, late 1960s, unmarked, rarely found with turkey finial. **$45-$55**

Globe jar, cold-painted details, 1960, McCoy USA mark. **$250-$300**

Granny with Glasses jar, on the left is the model used to make molds, and the production jar is at right, 1970s, USA mark. (Also found in white with gold trim.) **$90-$110**

Grapes jar with bird on lid in air-brushed colors, non-production piece, McCoy mark, 9 1/2" tall. **$7,000+**

Hamm's Bear jar, early 1970s, USA mark, also found with white tie. **$225-$250**

Harley Hog bank, 1984, HD McCoy mark but not made by McCoy, also found with decal and contrasting cap. **$90-$110**

Hen on Nest, late 1950s, USA mark, cold-painted details. **$90-$110**

Hobnail jars, stoneware, in yellow and hard-to-find cobalt, early 1940s, unmarked, note difference in lid configurations. **$100-$125 each**

Hobnail jars, stoneware, in blue and hard-to-find coral, early 1940s, unmarked.
$100-$125 each

Top: Two Hobnail Heart jars, in yellow and blue, early 1940s, unmarked.
$300-$350 each
Center: Two Hobnail Heart jars in streaky blue and pink, early 1940s, unmarked. **$300-$350 each**
Bottom: Two Hobnail Heart jars in matte white and lavender, early 1940s, unmarked. **$300-$350 each**

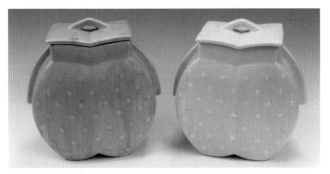

Hocus Rabbit jar, late 1970s, also found in gray, and may be marked "McCoy USA LCC" or with Designer Accents logo. **$80-$90**

Honey Bear jar with all decoration under glaze (some examples have cold paint), 1950s, McCoy USA mark. **$75-$90 for glazed** **$110-$125 for good cold paint**

Indian jar with cold-paint decoration, 1950s, McCoy mark.   **$200-$225**
At right is a model of the Indian jar, which was used to make a block from which the mold was cast.

Two commemorative Indian jars from the 1990s (slightly smaller than the originals), made by George Williams. Rick Wisecarver of Roseville, Ohio, painted the one on the right.
Left   **$150-$200**
Right   **$450-$550**

Jack-o'-Lantern jar, also comes with orange lid, late 1950s, McCoy USA mark. **$550-$650**

Kissing Penguins or Lovebirds, in typical factory cold paint decoration, 1940s, McCoy mark. (Rarely found in brown and green.) **$90-$110**

Left: Joey Kangaroo jar, late 1950s, McCoy USA mark. **$300-$350**
Right: Blue Kangaroo, mid-1960s, USA mark. **$225-$250**

McCoy POTTERY **33**

Left: Kittens on a Basket, 1950s, McCoy USA mark, cold-painted details, seldom found without damage to ears, so beware of restorations. **$450-$550**
Right: Kitten on Coal Bucket, 1983, McCoy USA LCC mark, also found with brown kitten on black bucket. **$200-$250**

Koala jar, 1980s, McCoy USA LCC mark.
$125-$150

Lamb on Basket-weave, 1950s, McCoy USA mark, cold-painted details. **$90-$110**

Lamb on Cylinder, 1950s, McCoy USA mark, cold-painted details. **$200-$225** (Also found with cats and dogs on lid.)

Lamb on Basket-Weave jar in atypical golden, green, and burgundy, 1950s, McCoy USA mark, all decoration under glaze. **$400-$500**

Lemon jar, 1970s. **$75-$85**

Liberty Bell jar, 1960s, unmarked, more common in silver than in bronze **$75-$90**

Little Clown jar, mid-1940s, McCoy mark, cold-painted details. **$80-$100**

Lollipop jar, late 1950s, McCoy USA mark, cold painted. **$70-$80**

Lunchbox jar, late 1980s, marked Designer Accents #377 USA. **$40-$50**
(Rarely found with green lid.)

Mammy jar in yellow, also found in white and aqua with cold paint decoration (widely available as a slightly smaller reproduction), 1950s, McCoy mark. **$200-$225** (Rarely found with two other phrases around base: "Dem Cookies Sure Am Good" and "Dem Cookies Sure Got Dat Vitamin A.")

Left: Reproduction Mammy jar; right, real Mammy jar with checked apron (paint touched up).

The following is from NM Xpress (http://www.members.aol.com/nmxpress/), Carol Seaman and Dan Eggert, Brecksville, Ohio:

McCoy Mammy: Original Mammy is a full 11" tall and comes in white, yellow, and aqua. The bottom is marked McCoy and is glazed with a dry foot. Details on some examples are cold painted on top of the glaze and show much wear. The reproduction jar is 10 1/4" tall, noticeably smaller all around. Unfortunately, it is marked the same and the cold-painted details can be scratched to look as if it has aged. Height is the best indicator to help authenticate the jar.

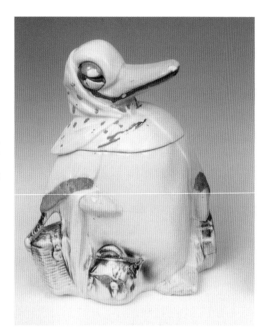

Mother Goose, late 1940s, McCoy USA mark, cold-painted details.

$90-$110

Nabisco jar, 1974, McCoy USA mark.

$70-$100

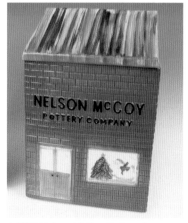

A 1999 Nelson McCoy Pottery Company jar, made in Crooksville, Ohio, as a commemorative, only 500 made.

$300-$350

Nursery Rhyme canister jars, early 1970s, unmarked, including Baa Baa Black Sheep, Humpty Dumpty, Little Bo Peep, Little Boy Blue, Little Miss Muffet, and Mary Mary Quite Contrary. **$75-$100 each**

Oak Leaf and Acorn corner jar (previously thought to have been produced by American Bisque), 1948, McCoy mark.
$200-$225

Mr. and Mrs. Owl jar, 1950s, McCoy USA mark, cold-painted details. **$90-$110**

Peanut Bird jar, late 1970s, unmarked.
$150-$175

A yellow and green Pear jar, 1950s, seen here with damage. Without damage.
$125-$150

Two versions of the Pear jar, both 1950s. The shorter jar on the left has pale yellow glaze and cold-painted leaves and stem.   **$100-$125 each**

Two more variations of the Pear jar. First, a blushing example with strong glaze on leaf knob and minimal burgundy glaze. Second, a flat-leaf pear with strong burgundy and yellow glaze.

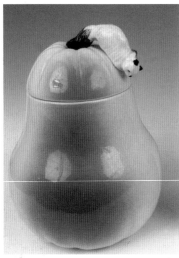

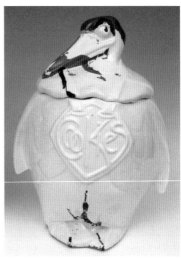

Lunch-hour piece, a Pear jar with a cat finial that was intended for use on a planter called "Pussy at the Well," 1950s.
$850-$1,000

Penguin jar, early 1940s, McCoy mark, typically found with worn cold paint, also found in yellow and pale green glaze.
$125-$150
(depending on paint condition)

Two Pepper jars in yellow and green, early 1970s to about 1980, either McCoy or McCoy USA marks, lids are not interchangeable, rarely found with textured glaze.
$45-$50 each

Picnic Basket jar, early 1960s, USA mark, with cold paint on the lid, 1960s. **$90-$110**

Pink Pig jar/bank, late 1970s, McCoy USA mark. **$90-$110**

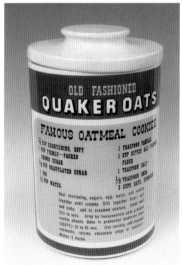

Quaker Oats jar, 1970, unmarked, not many McCoy examples, jar was later made by another company. **$500-$600**

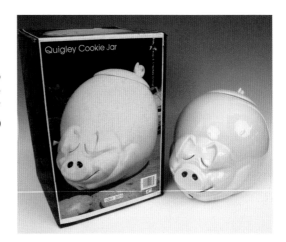

"Quigley" jar, also known as Lazy Pig, mid 1980s, USA mark, with original box.
$75-$100

Two versions of the Raggedy Ann jar, 1970s, USA mark. Left is painted with typical factory colors, right was hand-painted by a McCoy employee.
$90-$110 for factory colors

Sad Clown jar, early 1970s, unmarked, cold-painted details. **$90-$110**

Single Ear of Corn, 1958, McCoy USA mark, with good color match in the glaze, and with original label. **$125-$150**

Two views of a non-production Silhouette cookie jar with images of boy and girl hand-painted under the glaze (normally this form would have floral decoration), 1950s, missing lid, 6 1/2" tall. **No established value.**

Snow Bear jar, 1960s, McCoy USA mark, with cold-painted details.   **$75-$85**

Below left: Sweet Notes jar, now ac- knowledged to be McCoy, though that was once in doubt, with cold-paint deco- ration, 1950s.   **$600-$700**
Below right: Strawberries in a Basket, hard to find undamaged, late 1970s.
$150-$200

Strawberry jar, 1950s, Mc-Coy USA mark.
$80-$100

Teddy and Friend holiday variation, hand-painted at home in Christmas colors by a McCoy employee, late 1980s.
Because of paint **$175-$225**
Normally **$75-$100**

Left: reproduction Tepee jar; right: original Tepee jar, late 1950s, McCoy USA mark, straight top, cold-paint decoration, 11" tall.   **$250-$300**

Two styles of the Tepee jar, late 1950s, McCoy USA mark, slant top (left) and straight top, cold-paint decoration, 11" tall.   **$275-$325** for slant top

Thinking Puppy, late 1970s, USA mark. (Rarely found in tan or yellow.) **$40-$50**

Tulip Flowerpot jar, late 1950s, McCoy USA mark, found in other color combinations. **$125-$150**

Left: Touring Car jar in rare all black with gold trim, early 1960s, McCoy USA mark. **$200-$225**

Right: Touring Car in more common black and white with cold-painted details. **$100-$125**

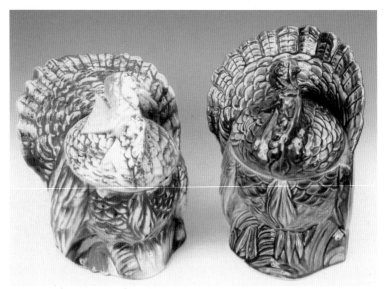

1940s, later in about 1960, brown with cold-painted wattle is more common. (Look for variations in label around turkey's neck.) **$175-$200**
Green glaze is harder to find and has no cold paint. **$250-$300**

Left: Turkey jar in white with all cold-paint decoration, 1940s. Depending on paint condition. **$250-$300**
Right: McCoy Limited Turkey bell (part of a set of seven with varying motifs), 1990s. **$70-$80**

Uncle Sam's Hat, mid-1970s, unmarked, hard to find. **$700-$800**

W.C. Fields jar, 1972, USA mark.
$200-$250

Wedding jar, 1960s, McCoy USA mark.
$90-$110

Windmill jar, 1961, McCoy USA mark, note color variation between lid and jar. **$70-$110,** depending on color match

Two versions of the Winking Pig jar, early 1970s, USA mark, typically found with cold-painted details. Yellow example is unusual. **$200-$250**

Wishing Well jar, 1960s, McCoy USA mark. **$50-$60**

Woodsy Owl jar and bank, 1970s, USA mark on jar, cold-painted details.
Jar   **$250-$300**
Bank   **$90-$110**

Wren House jar with "V" top, in an atypi-cal realistic glaze, early 1960s, McCoy USA mark, 9 1/2" tall. As shown with V top.   **$1,800-$2,000**
"V" top in normal colors   **$600-$700**

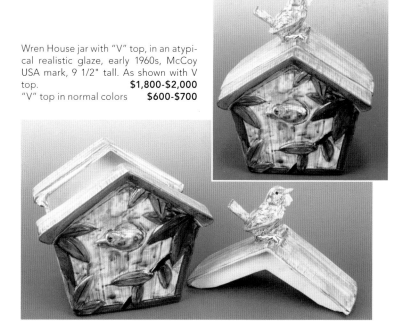

Moloney Collection Features Rare McCoy Cookie Jars

All the jars assembled are McCoy, from the collection of Kathleen Maloney of New York City.

Tony Veller: Probably the most highly prized of all McCoy cookie jars.
$10,000+

Leprechaun: Five versions of a rare jar. It was not produced, but unfortunately it has been reproduced. **$2,000-$5,000,** depending on color

Bareheaded Cookie Boy: Two versions of a rare jar, never produced. (The expressions on the boys' faces are quite different.) **$4,000+**

Turtle: This jar was never produced either, and we only know of two of them for sure. For a while, there was some question that it was made by McCoy. Recently, though, an original Cope sketch of the jar was discovered at the Cope Gallery. Mystery solved. **$7,500**

Fox Squirrel: Four versions of a rare jar. It's not as rare as we once thought, but it's pretty hard to find. The two hand-painted ones are painted over the glaze. There is one in the Cope Gallery with paint under the glaze.

$500 - $3,500 each for brown glazed squirrels

Dem Cookies Mammy: There are many variations of the Mammy cookie jar. This one is the most sought after of all, because along the base it says, "Dem Cookies sho got dat Vitamin A." This version was not produced. This one, in a beautiful matte aqua, is supposedly one of only two in existence. **$4,000**

Blue Train: This was designed in 1986 but was never produced. There are a couple versions in red and at least one in gray, but this may be the only one in blue. **$2,500**

Pine Cones: The base is the same as Mr. and Mrs. Owl jar, but the lid was an experiment. It was not produced and is possibly one of a kind. One side says Cookies, the other "When Shadows Fall." **$2,500**

Indian: Left example is hard to find. Right example was possibly one of a kind. It looks like the one on the left but does not have the word "Cookies" on the base. Supposedly the non-Cookies version was produced as a prototype for Pontiac, which then decided it didn't want it after all. McCoy changed it a bit (i.e., added the word Cookies) and produced it.

Left   **$200**
Right   **$3,000**

Forbidden Fruit: A common jar in a very unusual glaze. **$300**

Apple: A common jar in a very unusual glaze. **$250**

Keebler Treehouse: This is the earliest version, with applied (three-dimensional) decorations, not decals. The version that was mass-produced had decals. **$250**

Wren House: The one on the far left has a "split top." It's far more rare and sought after than the other two.
Left: $1,800; others, $600-$700

Jack-o'-Lantern: The one with the green top is marginally rarer and more popular than the other.
$550-$650 each

Penguin: The three colors. **$125-$150 each**

Stagecoach: The one on the left and the one on the right are the same except for the decorations. The one on the right is decorated completely under glaze, while the one on the left has some cold paint. The one in the center was made from a different mold. It is generally thought to be McCoy, but we're not sure.
$700-$800 each

Flowerpot with Tulip: This comes in red and yellow versions. As you can see, there is also a variation in the tulip finial. **$200**

White Turkey: There are three versions of the Turkey, multicolored, green, and white—all of them uncommon but mass produced. This one is pictured because it has been hand-decorated under the glaze. Decorators at the factory did this once in a while, as a gift for a family member or friend. This one appears to say, "The Lasiters." The decorated Football Boy is another good example of these lunch hour specials. **$300**

Football Boy: The standard Football Boy is pictured on the right. The one on the left has been customized, with the colors of the Crooksville Ceramics, and the name and number (on the back) of one of the players. There are others of these around in different school colors.

Left	**$500**
Center and right	**$150 each**

The Koala: The standard (and fairly common) Koala is on the left. The one on the right is marked "Sample" on the bottom and is done in an unusual glaze.

Standard glaze	**$100**
Atypical glaze	**$300**

Kissing Penguins: The standard jar (which is also called Lovebirds) is on the right. There are several unusual color variations out there, including one in a variegated green. This one is solid black.

Left	**$1,000**
Right	**$100**

Cat on a Coal Bucket: There are two versions of the jar, which was produced but is not terribly common. **$200-$250**

Cookie House: A popular jar, along with the two others in the "set": the Bank and the Cabin. **$200+**

Bear with Cookies in Vest: The most common version of this not hard-to-find jar is glazed white and decorated with cold paint. In this picture, the one on the right is yellow and decorated mostly with cold paint over the glaze. The decorations on the Bear on the left are almost all under glaze. Both are pretty hard to come by. **$250-$450 each**

Grandfather Clock: The simple brown on the right is the easiest to find of the three. On the left, you have the butterscotch covered (partially) with silver. In the center is green. **$200+ each**

The McCoy Cookie Bank cookie jar was created in the image of a real bank, and it's right on Main Street in Roseville, Ohio. When Leslie Cope designed the wonderful jar, produced in 1961 and usually considered one of a set of three, along with the Cookie Cabin and Cookie House, he used this handsome local bank as a model. **$110 each**

Flowerpot with Plastic Flowers: It was produced, but it's pretty rare. Sometimes you see one with obviously replaced flowers. **$200+**

Rooster: The two versions, both produced. **$75 each**

Basketball: Last but definitely not least, this is a jar that was not produced. There are at least three around (remember, if they made one, they probably made six; if they made six, they probably made12), and the two I've seen are decorated very differently. **$4,000**

Christmas Tree: The two versions: one silver, one gold. This was produced but is not easy to find. It's very popular. **$750-$1,000 each**

Crocks

Crocks and jugs are some of the earliest examples of McCoy wares, and those with salt-glazed surfaces and stenciled lettering are among the most prized.

Three white crocks with stenciled shield and "M" mark, in 8-, 12-, and 20-gallon sizes.
$125-$150

Three brown-top miniatures: plain crock, pickling crock, and jug. **$175-$225**

W. F. McCoy 5-gallon crock, salt glaze with stenciled ink lettering: "W.F. McCoy Wholesale Dealer in Stoneware–Zanesville, O.," with impressed "5," late 1800s, 13" tall.
In mint condition
$1,200-$1,400

W. F. McCoy 1 1/2-gallon crock, salt glaze with stenciled ink lettering: "W.F. McCoy Wholesale Dealer in Stoneware–Zanesville, O.," late 1800s, 9 1/4" tall.   **$1,000-$1,200**

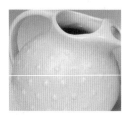

Dinnerware

This section includes pieces used for serving, eating, and drinking. Pieces used to prepare, cook, and store food are found in Kitchenware.

McCoy advertised "New! Ovenproof Suburbia Ware!" in this undated Creations in Ceramics promotion.

Platters, Casseroles & Baking Dishes

KITCHEN ACCESSORIES

28-9370

28-9371

28-0127-62

28-0126-62

28-9375

28-9374

28-0321-01

28-9380-01

28-9381-01

28-0326-01

28-0320-01

28-0326-01

28-0322-01

The Nelson McCoy Pottery Company
Subsidiary of Mount Clemens China Company
Roseville, Ohio 43777

Page 10

28-0326-01

Serving platters for turkey, chicken, and fish, along with some fondue pots, were displayed in a 1972 McCoy catalog.

Bunnies baby set (cup not shown), late 1970s, McCoy LCC mark with serial numbers 1221 and 1222, plate 6" diameter.   **$35-$40 as shown**

Above: Ball pitcher in cobalt blue, 1940s, NM mark or unmarked, 6" tall.
$50-$75

Ball pitcher with ice lip and four goblet-style tumblers in glossy burgundy, 1940s, unmarked.
Pitcher, 8 1/2" tall.   **$50-$60**
Tumblers, 5" tall.   **$25-$30 each**

Below: Four goblet-style tumblers in yellow, cobalt blue, aqua, and burgundy.   **$25-$30 each**

Two biscuit jars in glossy cobalt blue and yellow (with cold-paint stripes), 1930s, unmarked. **$75-$90 each**

Left: Biscuit or grease jar in glossy burgundy, 1950s, unmarked. **$90-$110**
Right: Suburbia creamer in glossy green, 1960s, McCoy USA mark, 5 1/2" tall. **$45-$55**

Tall Boot stein, 1970s, unmarked, 8" tall. **$25-$30**

Buttermilk pitcher in glossy yellow, late 1920s, unmarked or with shield, usually found in green, sometimes in caramel-tan, 5 1/2" tall. **$60-$70**

Bean pot, 1950s, McCoy mark, 6" tall. **$65-$75**

Biscuit or cracker jar, glossy maroon, 1930s. **$75-$90**

Covered butter dish in glossy green, 1960s, McCoy USA mark. **$30-$40**

Below left: Cabbage salt & pepper shakers with cork stoppers, 1950s, McCoy USA mark, 4 1/2" tall. **$75-$85/pair**
Below right: Cabbage grease jar, 1950s, McCoy USA, 9" tall. **$125-$150**

Above: Covered casserole, 1940s, McCoy USA, 6 1/2" diameter. **$55-$65**

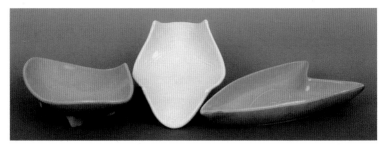

Three different 1960s candy dishes, McCoy USA mark. **$25-$35 each**

A sampling of Canyon ware, late 1970s, which included 28 pieces.
$30-$35/three-piece setting

Cherries and Leaves serving bowl, two individual salad bowls, and two cups, all in glossy aqua, mid-1930s, unmarked, all very rare. Serving bowl, 9" diameter
$450-$550
Salad bowls, 5" diameter **$225-$275 each**
Cups, 2 7/8" tall **$90-110 each**

Cherries and Leaves charger, 11 1/4" diameter, and individual salad bowl, 5" diameter, both in glossy yellow.
Bowl **$225-$275**
Charger **$5550-$650**

Cherries and Leaves charger in glossy yellow, mid-1930s, unmarked, 11 1/4" diameter. **$550-$650**

Left: Three Cherries and Leaves teapots in glossy burgundy, yellow, and aqua, mid-1930s, unmarked. **$90-$110 each**

Right: Cherries and Leaves teapot, creamer, and sugar in glossy blue (sometimes called plum), mid-1930s, unmarked.
Teapot only **$90-$110**
Creamer and sugar **$90-$110/pair**

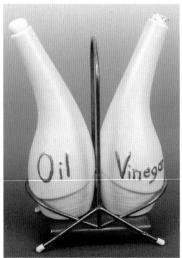

Cucumber and "Mango" salt & pepper shakers with cork stoppers, 1950s, McCoy USA mark, 5 1/4" tall.
$90-$110/pair

Above: Oil and vinegar cruets with original stand, mismatched stoppers, part of the "Citro-Ramics" line, early 1960s (originally sold for $1.60) McCoy USA mark, ex-Ty Kuhn collection, 9" tall plus stand. **$125-$150/pair**
Right: El Rancho Chuck Wagon food warmer, with wire base, 1960s, unmarked, 12" long. **$175-$200**

Christmas covered sugar, 1970s. **$35-$45**

Smile America mug, 1976. **$18-$22**

Six Boy Scouts of America mugs commemorating annual events, some dated (here, 1970s), hundreds of variations with transfer decoration. **$5-$10**

Two Bicentennial mugs, USA mark. **$15+**

Five variations of the Smiling Face mugs, 1970s, McCoy mark, 4" tall. **$15-$20 each**

Below: Six sports-theme mugs, late '80s, unmarked, 4" to 4 1/2" tall. **As a set $150** Individual mugs may be valued at **$30**.

Gorilla mug, late 1970s, McCoy LCC mark, 4 1/2" tall. **$25-$35**

Two Cloverleaf pitchers with open ice lip, late 1940s, McCoy USA mark, 7" tall. **$45-$55 each**

Elephant and Donkey pitchers (also called pitcher vases) in matte white, 1940s, NM USA mark, rare in any color. **$300-$350 each**

Two Donkey pitchers (also called pitcher vases) in glossy green and white, 1940s, NM USA mark, rare in any color. **$300-$350 each**

Left: Donkey pitcher in glossy aqua, 1940s, NM USA mark. **$300-$350**
Right: Elephant pitcher in rare burgundy, 1940s, NM USA mark. **$4,000**

Two Fish pitchers (also called a pitcher vase), late 1940s, McCoy mark.
$900-$1,000 each

Grecian teapot, creamer and sugar, 1950s, McCoy USA mark and style number 455, teapot 8" tall with lid.
$125-$150/set

Three Hobnail ice jugs, in yellow, coral, and blue, early 1940s, unmarked.

$150-$175 each

Two Hobnail ice-lip pitchers in glossy burgundy and cobalt blue, 1940s, NM mark and unmarked, 6" tall. **$50-$75 each**

Two Hobnail ice-lip pitchers in matte aqua and lavender, 1940s, NM mark or unmarked, 6" tall.

$50-$75 each

Two Hobnail pitchers in glossy yellow and lavender, 1940s, NM mark or unmarked, note difference in lip hole sizes, 6" tall. **$50-$75 each**

Ivy teapot, creamer, and sugar in gold trim, 1950s, McCoy USA mark, rarely found in yellow and black.
$275-$325/set

Parading Ducks pitcher, holds 4 pints, late 1930s, stoneware, unmarked.
$125-$150 each

Two Parading Ducks pitchers in glossy brown and burgundy, holds 4 pints, late 1930s, stoneware, unmarked, found in a variety of colors.
$125-$150 each

Two Parading Ducks pitchers in glossy yellow and aqua, holds 4 pints, late 1930s, stoneware, unmarked, found in a variety of colors.
$125-$150 each

Two Parrot pitchers (also called pitcher vases), early 1950s, McCoy USA mark. **$200-$225 each**

Above: Miniature Pig pitchers, 1997 from the McCoy Collection, right example in non-production glaze, 6 1/2" tall.
$45-$55 each
Left: Miniature Pig pitcher, not a production piece but marked McCoy, 5 1/2" tall. **$500+**

Pine Cone creamer and sugar in gold trim probably done by McCoy, 1950s, McCoy mark. **$70-$80/pair**

Pine Cone teapot, creamer and sugar, 1950s, McCoy mark. **$125-$150/set**

Pitcher and two mugs in green and yellow, 1920s, stoneware, these shapes also found in barrel motif, 9" and 5" tall.

Pitcher   **$100-$125**
Mugs   **$30-$35 each**

Also, four mugs displayed in a metal rack.

Pitcher and mugs in the Grape pattern in brown and white, late 1920s, stoneware, unmarked, commonly found in green.

Pitcher, 8 1/2" tall **$80-$90**
Mugs, 5" tall   **$20-$25**

(Produced at the same time was the Buccaneer pitcher and mugs, almost always in green with shield mark #6 on the mugs, in about the same price range.)

Ring Ware pitcher and three tumblers in glossy green (note color variations), 1920s, unmarked.

Pitcher, 9" tall **$80-$100**
Tumblers, 4 1/4" tall
                $80-$90 each

McCoy POTTERY **83**

Strap pitcher in glossy burgundy, late 1940s, Mc-Coy mark. **$75-$85**

Soup and sandwich set, 1960s, McCoy USA on both, found in other colors. **$25-$35/set**

Two strap-handle (also called dusk's neck handle) Berry pitchers in glossy brown and green, 1930s, unmarked. **$90-$110 each**

Two Stoneware pitchers in green (common, also found in yellow) and burgundy, late 1920s, unmarked.
Left: 7" tall **$65-$80**
Right: 7 3/4" tall
$90-$110

Left: W.C. Fields pitcher (came packaged with decanter), 1970s, 7" tall. **$45-$55**

Right: Non-production Grapes-motif pitcher in matte blue, marked with conjoined "TK" (Ty Kuhn), 7" tall. **$50-$60**

Three Water Lily pitchers with Fish handles in tan and white, mid-1930s, unmarked. 7", **$85-$100** 5 1/2" **$60-$70** (not commonly found in white)

Left: Water Lily pitcher with Fish handle in glossy green, mid-1930s, unmarked, 5 1/2" tall. **$60-$70**
Right: Bird and Cherries pitcher, mid-1930s, unmarked, 5" tall. **$45-$55**

Experiments

Experimental pieces often served as tests for new glazes and may have inscribed number and letter codes. Though not common, they can be difficult to value since there is little basis for comparison. Still, collectors prize them as production oddities.

Below: Blue and tan glaze on a baluster vase; right: part of an Apple wall pocket with burgundy glaze; ex-Ty Kuhn collection, with glaze marks. **$60-$70 each**

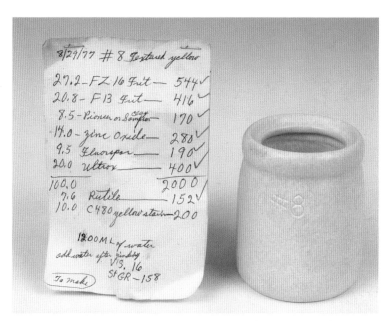

Above: Small jar with textured yellow glaze, inscribed #8, with glaze formula written by Ty Kuhn.
$70-$90

Two 3" flower pots with speckled beige and blue glazes, inscribed on the bottom with glaze numbers, ex-Ty Kuhn collection. **$50-$60 each**

Bottom of pitcher flower holder done in a test glaze with the mark, "X 79," which was a glossy coral. **$150-$200**

Two mini jugs, the left marked "#3 bamboo," the right with eagle decal, 5 1/2" tall, ex-Ty Kuhn collection.
$40-$50 each

Left: Planter in dark olive glaze, Lancaster Colony, ex-Ty Kuhn collection. **$35-$40**
Right: A pair of chafing dishes in forest green glaze, ex-Ty Kuhn collection. **$40/pair**

Two Basket-weave pots and saucers, 3" and 4", in atypical purple and blue-green glazes, ex-Ty Kuhn collection. **$35-$40 each**

Pitcher, hand-painted by Betty Ford, known for painting apples and roosters on Watt Ware pieces, 6" tall. **$75** This pitcher in factory glaze. **$45**

Left and below: Shell soap dishes in various trial glazes, with either a tripod foot or three button feet, late 1970s.
$30-$35 each

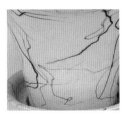

Flowerpots

Flowerpots have a devoted following among McCoy collectors. While many pots are simple and unadorned utilitarian pieces, the challenge has become finding them in their various sizes and glazes. Many pots are unmarked, but familiarity with designs and glazes helps with attribution.

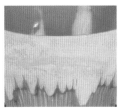

The Harmony line of flowerpots and vases featured "hand decorated modernistic designs," according to McCoy.

33-0541-46

50-0552-06

50-0551-06

Green Thumb

44-0393-01

44-0392-01

44-0389-01

44-0388-01

44-0377-01

44-0376-01

44-0378-01

31-3010-01

50-0532-13

44-0386-17

27

Among McCoy's largest lines of flowerpots was the Green Thumb line in many shapes and sizes.

Two Brick pots in matte aqua, early 1940s, NM USA mark. 7" tall
4 1/4" tall

$100-$120
$65-$75

Butterfly Line pot and saucer in matte aqua and yellow, 1940s, NM USA mark, 6 1/2" diameter.

$75-$85

Four Butterfly Line pots and saucers in matte blue, coral, aqua, and yellow, 1940s, NM USA mark, 3 1/4" diameter. **$55-$65 each**
(Note variation in mold crispness; a sharp mold can add to the price.)

Above: Three Dragonfly pots, two with saucers, in matte white, 1940s, unmarked.

3 1/2" tall	**$40-$50**
4 1/2" tall	**$50-$60**
5 1/2" tall	**$60-$70**

Left: Two Dragonfly pots and saucers in matte coral and yellow, 1940s, unmarked, 3 1/2" diameter. **$60-$70 each**

Two Leaves and Berries flowerpots in matte white, unmarked, 4 1/2" and 5" diameter. **$45-$55**

Leaves and Berries flowerpot in matte brown and green, 5 1/2" diameter. **$60-$70**

Three Quilted Rose pots and saucers in matte white, unmarked 3", 5", and 5 1/2" tall. **$40-$50 each**

Two Sand Dollar pots and saucers in matte white, 1940s, unmarked, 4" and 6" tall. **$40-$50 each** (Note difference in mold details: The left is crisp and the right is soft.)

Two sizes of the "Viney" pots, one with saucer, in matte white, 1930s, un-marked.
9" tall   **$125-$150**
5" tall   **$70-$80**

Left: Leafy flowerpot in glossy ivory glaze, late 1940s, unmarked, 7" tall. **$110-$125**
Right: Ivy pot in matte white, 1930s, unmarked, 6" tall. **$50-$60**

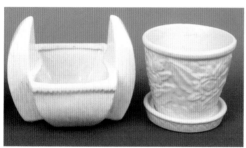

Left: Bulb planter (also called "the Viking helmet") in glossy white, 1950s, 5" tall. **$50-$60**
Right: pot and saucer in matte white, 1930s, unmarked, 4" tall. **$25-$30**

Three Roses on a Wall pots and saucers in glossy green, 1950s, McCoy mark, also found in pink, white, and yellow. From left, 3 7/8", 5", 4 1/4" tall. **$25-$45 each**

Three textured pots and saucers in glossy green, 1950s, McCoy mark. From left, 3", 5", and 4" tall. **$25-$45 each** (with the smallest being the most expensive)

Two Icicles pots and sau-
cers in yellow and green,
1950s, McCoy mark, un-
glazed border is easily
soiled and tough to clean,
4 1/2" and 3 7/8" tall.
$25-$30 each

Pot with test glazes ap-
plied, ex-Ty Kuhn collec-
tion, 5" tall.   **$150-$200**

Three sizes of flowerpots
in pale green, 1950s, Mc-
Coy USA mark, 7", 6 1/4",
and 4 1/4" tall.
$75-$100 each

Three Dragonfly pots and
saucers in matte blue
(sometimes called "but-
terfly blue) and aqua,
1940s, unmarked.
6" diameter   **$90-$110**
5" diameter   **$75-$85**
3 1/2" diameter **$60-$70**

Two pots in atypical glossy tan glaze. Left, 1930s, McCoy mark, 6" tall. **$35-$45** Right, 1940s, unmarked, 4 1/2" tall. **$25-$35**

Two Green Thumb pots and saucers, 1970s, Mc-Coy USA mark with style numbers 0375 and 0373, 6" and 5" tall.
$20-$25 each

Three Basket-weave and Leaves pots and saucers in matte yellow, aqua, and blue, 1940s, NM USA mark, 5 1/2" tall.
$50-$60 each

Two Basket-weave and Leaves pots and saucers in matte blue and yellow, 1940s, NM USA mark, 7 1/2" tall. **$65-$75 each**

Three sizes of Hobnail pots and saucers in matte yellow and white, 1940s, NM USA mark.

6" tall	**$90-$110**
5" tall	**$60-$70**
3 3/4" tall	**$50-$60**

Two Hobnail and Leaves pots and saucers in matte white and blue, 1940s, NM USA mark, 4" and 3 1/2" tall. **$50-$60 each**

Three sizes of Ribbed pots and saucers in matte green, green and brown, and white, 1930s, unmarked.

6" tall	**$90-$110**
5" tall	**$80-$90**
4" tall	**$60-$70**

Three sizes of Lily Bud pots and saucers in matte blue, rose, and yellow, 1940s, NM USA mark.

6" tall	**$65-$75**
5" tall	**$50-$60**
3 1/2" tall	**$40-$50**

Four sizes of Leaf and Flowers pots and saucers in glossy burgundy, matte green and brown, and matte white, 1930s, stoneware, unmarked.

7" tall	**$125-$150 (less for other matte colors)**
6" tall	**$65-$75**
5" tall	**$50-$60**
4" tall	**$60-$70**

Three sizes of Hobnail and Leaves pots and saucers in glossy yellow, green, and blue, 1940s, McCoy USA mark.

6" tall	**$65-$75**
5" tall	**$55-$65**
3 1/2" tall	**$45-$55**

Four sizes of Flat-Leaf pots and saucers in glossy blue and burgundy, and matte green, 1940s, unmarked.

6 1/2" tall	**$90-$110**
5 1/2" tall	**$80-$90**
4" tall	**$65-$75**
3" tall	**$65-$75**

Three sizes of Reeded pots and saucers in matte yellow, coral, and blue, 1940s, NM USA mark.

6" tall	**$65-$75**
5" tall	**$55-$65**
4" tall	**$45-$55**

Three Lotus Leaf pots and saucers (sometimes saucer is detached) in glossy tan and green, matte brown and green, and glossy green, 1930s, unmarked.

6" tall	**$75-$85**
4" tall	**$50-$60**

Lotus Leaf pot and saucer (detached) in brown and green, 1930s, unmarked, 10" tall. **$350-$450**

Below: Three sizes of pots and saucers in matte white and pink, early 1960s, Mc-Coy USA mark.

6" tall	**$40-$50**
5" tall	**$35-$40**
4" tall	**$30-$35**

Two Basket-weave with Rings pots and saucers in glossy burgundy and green, 1950s, unmarked.
6" tall **$75-$85**
4" tall **$50-$60**

Two pots and saucers (detached) in glossy cobalt blue and green, 1940s, unmarked, 6 1/2" and 5" tall. **$65-$75 each**

Large pot and saucer (detached) in glossy yellow, late 1930s, unmarked, 11" tall. **$160-$175**

Pot and saucer (detached) in glossy burgundy, 1940s, unmarked, 9 1/2" tall. **$125-$150**

Four textured pots and saucers in glossy pink, green, brown, and yellow, late 1950s, McCoy mark.

6" tall	**$45-$55**
5" tall	**$35-$40**
4" tall	**$30-$35**
3" tall	**$20-$25**

Two Sand Dollar pots and saucers (sometimes referred to as "NECCO" style, after the round wafer cookie) in glossy green and yellow, 1930s, unmarked.

6" tall	**$55-$65**
4" tall	**$45-$55**

Four assorted pots in glossy cobalt blue and burgundy, matte green, and glossy yellow, 3" to 4" tall. **$35-$45 each** (Cobalt blue pot at left is attributed to McCoy.)

Two Garden Club pots and saucers in matte green, late 1950s, McCoy USA mark.

5 1/2" tall	**$55-$65**
3 1/2" tall	**$45-$55**

Garden Club pot and sau-
cer in glossy yellow, late
1950s, McCoy USA mark,
8" tall. **$80-$90**

Garden Club pot in glossy
turquoise, late 1950s, Mc-
Coy USA mark, 9" tall.
$80-$90

Garden Club pot and sau-
cer in glossy green, late
1950s, McCoy USA mark,
7 1/4" tall. **$65-$75**

Two Hobnail pots and
saucers with stylized
Greek key bands in glossy
pink and yellow, 1940s,
McCoy mark, 5" and 4"
tall. **$30-$40 each**

Two "Squiggle" pots and saucers in glossy yellow and matte pink, 1960s, McCoy USA
mark, 5 1/2" tall. **$50-$60**

Two Quilted pots and saucers in glossy green and yellow, 1950s, McCoy USA mark, 5" tall and 4" tall. **$30-$35 each**

Two Quilted Roses pots and saucers in glossy pink and brown, 1950s, McCoy USA mark, 5" tall.
$65-$75 each

Two Daisy pots and saucers, 1950s, McCoy USA mark.
6 1/2" tall   **$65-$75**
4" tall   **$45-$55**

Two matte brown pots, one with saucer, late 1970s, McCoy LCC mark, 4 1/2" and 5" tall.
$40-$50 each

Three assorted pots and saucers in glossy green and yellow, and matte brown and green, 1930s, unmarked, 3" to 4" tall. **$40-$60 each**
(Green pot is attributed to McCoy.)

Two Swirl pots and saucers in semi-gloss green, 1950s, McCoy USA mark, 6" and 4" **$25-$35 each**

Two Speckled pots and saucers in glossy turquoise and pink, 1950s, McCoy USA mark, 6" and 4" tall. **$25-$35 each**

Two Fish-scale pots and
saucers in glossy blue and
yellow, 1940s, NM USA
mark. 7" tall. **$55-$65**
4" tall **$40-$45**

Below: Three Reeded
pots and saucers in semi-
gloss pink, yellow, and
green, 1940s, NM USA
mark.
6" tall, **$55-$65**
5" tall **$45-$55**
4" tall **$35-$40**

Two Brocade Line pots
and saucers in pink and
black and pink and green,
1950s, McCoy USA mark,
6" tall. **$50-$60 each**

Three pots and saucers, McCoy USA marks. Left and right, 3" tall.   **$20-$30 each**
Center, Icicles in blue, 6 1/2" tall.   **$40-$50**

Two pots and saucers. Left, glossy turquoise, 1930s, unmarked, 6" tall.   **$65-$75**
Right, Ring Ware in glossy green, 1930s, unmarked,
5 1/2" tall.   **$75-$85**

Pot in test glaze, ex-Ty
Kuhn collection.   **$100+**

Butterfly line pot, 1940s,
NM USA mark, 4 1/2 in
tall.   **$45-$55**

Jardinières and Pedestals

From the earliest blended and matte glazes made just after the turn of the 19th century to the late incarnations of the 1970s, "jards and peds" (as collectors call them) are a challenging area for treasure hunters trying to match tops and bottoms. Many are unmarked.

The 1958 McCoy catalog featured a variety of jardinières, as well as a porch jar.

Jardinieres   Jardinieres & Peds
Pet Feeders

No. 421C—4" Sq. Jardiniere
Amethyst inside—Pink outside
Mustard inside—Brown outside
Packed 1 Doz. Wt. 25 lbs.
$14.40 per Dozen

No. 412—7½" Jardiniere
Brown Spray or Green Spray
Packed 1 Doz. Wt. 42 lbs.
$17.60 per Dozen

No. 45—7½" Jardiniere
Yellow or White
Packed 1 Doz. Wt. 52 lbs.
$14.40 per Dozen

No. 58 Jardiniere
Sizes 4½"-5½"-6½"-7½"-
8½"-9½"-10½"
Green, White, Yellow
4½"—$ 6.70 per Doz.   1 Doz. 37 lbs.
5½"—$ 8.40 per Doz.   1 Doz. 40 lbs.
6½"—$10.20 per Doz.   1½ Doz. 42 lbs.
7½"—$14.40 per Doz.   1½ Doz. 42 lbs.
8½"—$20.00 per Doz.   2/3 Doz. 37 lbs.
9½"—$24.60 per Doz.   2/3 Doz. 50 lbs.
10½"—$32.00 per Doz.   1/3 Doz. 36 lbs.

No. 48—Jardiniere
Sizes 8½"-10½"
Green or White
8½"—$20.00 per Doz.   2/3 Doz. 47 lbs.
10½"—$32.00 per Doz.   1/3 Doz. 40 lbs.

No. 49—Jar and Ped.
Green and White
8½" Jard. and 12½" Pedestal
1 only—15 lbs.
$5.30 each

No. 5—10" Porch Jar
White or Green
Packed 1/3 Doz. Wt. 17 lbs.
Available with or without
Drainage—please specify
$4.00 each

The Irresistibles

"New" No. 1915
4 ¼" x 4 ¼"
Round Pedestal Planter
Green or Stoneware White

Nos. 1915-1916-1917
May Be Assorted.

No. 1916—4 ¼" x 4 ¼"
Round Pedestal Planter
Green or Stoneware White

No. 1917—4 ¼" x 4 ¼"
Swirl Pedestal Planter
Green or Stoneware White

No. 1310
11 ½" x 3 ½"
Aladdin Planter
Colors: Matte Green,
Matte White, Matte Black

No. 1176—6"

No. 1175—5"

No. 1174—4"

Colors: Butterscotch, Stoneware White, Jardiniere Green

No. 1488—Jardiniere
8 ½"—10 ½"
Green or White
No. 1488—8 ½"
No. 1480—10 ½"

No. 1888—Jardiniere
4 ½"-5 ½"-6 ½"-7 ½"-8 ½"-10 ½"
Stoneware White or Gloss Green

No. 1884—4 ½"	No. 1887— 7 ½"
No. 1885—5 ½"	No. 1888— 8 ½"
No. 1886—6 ½"	No. 1880—10 ½"

5

Jardinières and several styles of planters were among "The Irresistibles" in McCoy's marketing.

Jardinière and pedestal in glossy turquoise and cobalt blue drip glaze, circa 1910, 41" tall overall, unmarked.
$1,500-$2,000

Basket-Weave jardinière in matte yellow, 6 3/4" tall. **$70-$80**

Basket-Weave jardinière in matte aqua, 7 1/2" diameter. **$80-$100**

Basket-Weave jardinière and pedestal in matte white, jardinière 7 1/2" diameter, pedestal (NM USA mark) 13" tall. **$300-$350/pair**

Basket-Weave jardinière in matte brown and green, 1930s, unmarked, 9" tall.
$350-$450

Butterfly jardinière, matte yellow, 7" tall, NM mark.
$125-$150

Two Butterfly jardinières in matte white, both NM mark.

3 1/2" diameter	**$30-$40**
7 1/2" diameter	**$125-$150**

Holly jardinière in matte brown and green, 5" tall. **$40-$50**
Leaves and Berries flowerpot with saucer in matte brown and green,
4 1/2" tall. **$40-$50**

Three Holly jardinières in matte green.

5"	**$40-$50**
7 1/2"	**$80-$90**
4" diameter	**$30-$40**

Left and right, two 4" Leaves and Berries jardinières in matte green showing variations in color and mold crispness, 1930s, unmarked. **$35-$45**
A 5" Holly jardinière in matte green, 1930s, unmarked. **$45-$55**

Leaves and Berries jardinière and pedestal in matte green, jardinière 8 1/2" diameter, pedestal 12 1/2" tall.
$300-$400/pair

Holly jardinière and pedestal in matte green, unmarked, jardinière 7 1/2" diameter, pedestal 13" tall.
$300-$350/pair

Right: Leaves and Berries jardinière and pedestal in matte brown and green, jardinière 7 1/2" diameter, pedestal 6 3/4" tall.
$225-$275/pair
Far right: Leaves and Berries jardinière and pedestal in matte green, jardinière 7 1/2" diameter, pedestal 6 1/2" tall. **$225-$275/pair**

Leaves and Berries jardinière in matte brown and green, 1930s, unmarked, 4" diameter. **$50-$60**

Leaves and Berries jardinière and pedestal in matte white, jardinière 8 1/2" diameter, pedestal 12 3/4" tall. **$250-$300**

Lily Bud jardinière, 1940s, NM USA mark, 7 1/2" diameter. **$55-$65**

Oak Leaves and Acorns jardinière in matte green, late 1920s, unmarked, 6 3/4" tall. **$70-$80**

Oak Leaves and Acorns jardinière in matte green, 5" diameter, and Holly jardinière in matte green, 4" diameter. **$40-$50 each**

Quilted jardinière in matte white, 9" diameter. **$90-$100**
Oak Leaves and Acorns jardinière in matte white, 7 1/2" diameter. **$60-$70**

Quilted jardinière and pedestal in matte white, jardinière 7 1/2" diameter, pedestal (NM USA mark) 13" tall. **$250-$300**

Sand Butterfly jardinière, matte white, 7" tall. **$60-$70**

Sand Butterfly jardinières in brown and green.
8" diameter **$80-$90**
5" diameter **$40-$50**

Swallows jardinière in matte green, 1940s, unmarked, 5" tall. **$40-$50**

Swallows jardinière in matte green, 1940s, unmarked, 7 1/2" diameter. **$80-$90**

Swallows jardinières in matte white, 1940s, unmarked.
7 1/2" diameter **$90-$110**
4" diameter **$50-$60**

Two Oak Leaves and Acorns jardinières in matte white, late 1920s, unmarked.
6 1/2" tall **$70-$80**
4 1/4" tall **$45-$55**

Leaves and Berries jardinière and pedestal in matte white, 1930s, no mark; jardinière, 7 1/2" tall; pedestal, 13" tall.
$350-$450/pair
(In glossy blended glazes, add $100.)

Two Leaves and Berries straight-side jardinières in matte white, 1930s, unmarked.
6 1/2" tall   **$90-$110**
4 1/4" tall   **$50-$60**

Two Swallows jardinières in cobalt blue and matte white, 1940s, unmarked, 7" tall.   **$90-$110**
(with cobalt being slightly higher)

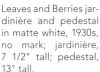

Left: Basket-weave jardinière in matte white, 1930s, NM mark or unmarked, 7 1/2" tall. Right: Morning Glory jardinière in matte white, late 1920s, unmarked, 6 1/2" tall.
$70-$80 each

Holly jardinière in matte white, 1930s, unmarked, 9" tall.
$175-$225

Ivy jardinière in brown and green, early 1950s, unmarked, also found in a brighter glossy tan and green with matching pedestal, 8" tall.
$350-$450

Sand Butterfly jardinière and pedestal in matte white, 1930s, unmarked; jardinière, 9" tall; pedestal, 13 1/4" tall.
$300-$350/pair

Smallest Swallows jardinière in matte blue, 1940s, unmarked, 4" tall.
$55-$65

Two hook jardinières in glossy burgundy, 1940s, NM mark or unmarked.
7 1/2"   **$50-$60**
4 1/2" diameter **$30-$40**

Fish in Net jardinière in rare gray-green, late 1950s, McCoy mark, also found in brown, 7 1/2" tall.   **$250-$300**

Jardinière in matte aqua, stoneware, in floral pattern, 1930s, unmarked, 7 1/2" tall. **$70-$80**

Two hook jardinières in glossy aqua, 1940s, NM mark or unmarked. 7 1/2" diameter **$50-$60**
3 3/4" diameter **$25-$30**

Two jardinières with applied leaves and berries, late 1940s, McCoy USA mark, 7 1/2" tall.
$200-$250 each
Below: Three sizes of Hobnail jardinières in matte aqua, 1940s, NM USA mark, found in other matte colors.
3" tall **$35-$40**
4" tall **$45-$50**
6 1/2" tall **$75-$85**

Two Grecian jardinières (5 1/2" and 4 1/2" tall), 1950s, McCoy USA mark and style number 443 on jardinières. **$50-$60 each**
(center) Grecian urn vase, 9 1/2" tall, 1950s. **$110-$125**

Sand Butterfly jardinière in matte aqua (rare color), stoneware, 1930s, unmarked, usually found white or in brown and green, 4" tall. **$55-$65**

Stained Glass jardinière, 1950s, Mc-Coy USA mark, 5" tall. **No established value.**

Butterfly Line pieces in matte aqua.
Left: Smallest jardinière, 1940s, NM USA mark, 3 1/4" diameter. **$45-$50**
Right: Square-top jardinière, USA mark, 3 3/4" square. **$55-$65**

Jardinière in matte white, 1950s, McCoy USA mark, 7" tall. **$50-$60**

Hook jardinière in matte white, 1940s, 3" tall. **$25-$35**

Two Butterfly Line pieces in matte aqua and yellow.
Left: Square-top footed jardinière, 1940s, USA mark, 5 1/4" square. **$110-$125**
Right: Square-top footed jardinière, 1940s, USA mark, 3 3/4" square. **$55-$65**

Jars

This section includes oil jars, porch jars (basically used as big planters), and sand jars (once common in hotel lobbies as receptacles for cigars and cigarettes). Some of the larger stoneware pieces were first made in the 1920s and '30s, but these same designs can still be found on McCoy catalog pages from the 1950s.

Cherries sand jar in matte white, 1930s, unmarked, 14" by 10". **$350-$450**

Low Sand Butterfly porch jar in matte white, 1930s, unmarked, 11" tall.
$150-$200

Porch jar with rings and grape motif in matte white, 1940s, NM mark, 9 1/4" tall.
$175-$225
Brown and green **$300-$400**

Oil jar in glossy aqua, late 1930s, NM mark, 12" tall.
$150-$200

Porch jar with tab handles in matte white, 1930s, unmarked, heights can vary from 17 3/8" to 18".
Matte white
No established value
Brown and green
$500-$600

Oil jar with hand-painted floral decoration by Betty Ford, 1940s, NM mark, 12" tall, with rim chip.
If perfect, **$150-$200**

Sand Butterfly porch jar in matte white, 1930s, unmarked, heights can vary from 19 1/2" to just over 20".
Matte white
No established value
Brown and green
$550-$650

Porch jar with grapes motif in matte aqua, late 1930s, stoneware, NM USA mark, 9 1/2" tall. **$250-$300**

Porch jar in matte aqua, with dense Leaves and Berries pattern and double ring handles, 1930s, unmarked, one of only three known, 11 1/2" tall.
$3,500-$4,500

Kitchenware

This section includes pieces used to prepare, cook, and store food. Pieces used for serving, eating, and drinking are found in Dinnerware.

The Wood & White line included a breadboard, condiment set, casserole, bowls, a coffee carafe, and salt & pepper shakers.

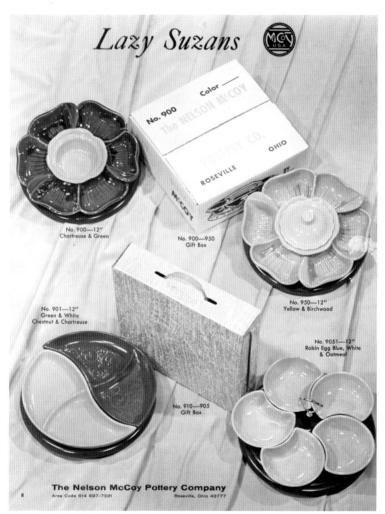

McCoy highlighted four styles and colors of Lazy Suzans in this promotion.

Two sizes of the batter bowl with spoon rest in glossy green, late 1920s, shield mark #3, diameters without spouts and handles.

7 1/2"   **$175-$225**
9 1/2"   **$275-$325**

Cook-Serve Ware covered casserole and stickhandle creamer, late 1940s, McCoy mark.
Casserole   **$35-$40**
Creamer   **$10-$15**

Two Ring ware covered vessels (casseroles?) in glossy green, note different sized knobs, 1920s, shield mark "M"; 3 5/8" and 4" tall not including lids.
$175-$200 each

Mixing bowl in the Wave or Sunrise pattern, size No. 7, from a set of six ranging in size from 5" to 11" diameter, 1920s, square bottom, also found in yellow and burgundy; and three 5" mixing bowls in green, yellow, and burgundy. Individual sizes range from **$175-$250 each.**
Complete set   about **$1,200**

Two square-bottom Ring ware mixing bowls in green and yellow, 1930s, shield mark with size inside (8" and 9", though they may actually be up to a half inch larger in diameter), also a pattern number (2, indicating the ring pattern).   **$150-$175 each**

Raspberries and Leaves mixing bowl in glossy white, 1930s, unmarked, 9" diameter. **$200-$225**

Three Raspberries and Leaves mixing bowls in teal, light burgundy, and blue, 1930s, unmarked, 9" diameter (there may be other sizes). **$200-$225 each**

Various sizes of mixing bowls with tiny berries in the outer rim and fluted bodies, 1930s, unmarked, sizes include 4", 6", 7", 8", priced in ascending sizes. **$35-$100**

Four mixing bowls in the Feather pattern in ivory, yellow, green, and burgundy, 1940s, McCoy mark, 6", 7", and 8" diameter. **$35-$75**

Two mixing bowls in glossy pink, 1950s, McCoy USA Oven Proof mark, 5" and 6" diameter.
$35-$45 each

Also found in other sizes.

Five sizes of Stone Craft mixing bowls (called pink and blue) ranging in diameter from 7" to 14" (also a 5" size), mid-1970s, McCoy LCC mark.
$225-$250/complete set

Penguin spoon rest, 1950s, 7" x 5 1/2".
$125-$175

Two Islander Line creamers in yellow and white, early 1980s. **$50-$60 each**

Ring ware hanging salt box and covered jar (cheese or butter), both in glossy green, 1920s, shield mark "M."
Salt box, 6" tall   **$250-$300**
Covered jar, 5" tall   **$175-$200**

Ring ware covered butter or cheese crock, 1920s, shield mark "M." **$90-$110**

Lamps

Many McCoy lamp bases are unmarked, so comparing glazes can be a clue to their origin. Look for oddities, like vase forms converted to lamps, and for figural bases with atypical glazes.

"Anniversary" or Sunflower lamp base in glossy white, 1930s, unmarked, 8 1/2" tall. **$50-$60**

Cowboy Boots lamp, 1950s, McCoy USA mark, with replacement shade, boots only 7" tall. **$75-$100**

Fireplace TV lamp/planter, 1950s, unmarked, also found in chartreuse and black, and with screen behind logs, 9" tall. **$90-$110**

Two Hyacinth lamps, made at the McCoy factory but not production pieces, early 1950s, McCoy mark, 8 1/2" tall (pottery only). **$1,800-$2,000 each**
The Hyacinth vases in these colors typically are valued at about **$150-$225**.

Mermaid TV lamp in gray and burgundy, 1950s, unmarked, also found in black and chartreuse, 9 1/2" tall. **$200-$250**

Lamp base in glossy streaked blue onyx glaze, sometimes found in matte glazes, with leafy borders and twig handles, 1940s, unmarked, 9" tall. **$300-$350**

Lamps

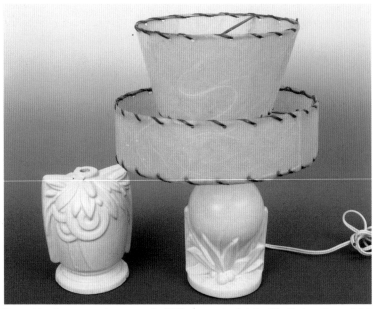

Two white Stoneware lamps, early 1940s, unmarked; left: Lily Bud pattern; right: Leaves and Berries; each 5 1/2" tall.   **$600-$700 each**

Left: Stoneware lamp in matte green, 1940s, 8 1/2" tall. **$350-$450**
Right: Fisherman or Whaling Man lamp base, 1950s, 16 1/4" tall (reproductions are slightly smaller). **$250-$300**
More with original wiring and hardware.

Two Sunflower lamps, one in blue-gray, one in burgundy, 1950s, also found in chartreuse, yellow, McCoy USA mark, 9" tall.   **$70-$90 each**

Arcature lamp with textured surface, 1950s, McCoy USA mark, base 9" tall.   **$110-$125**

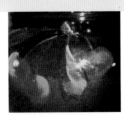

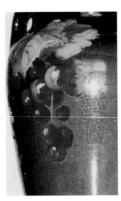

Loy-Nel-Art

The J.W. McCoy Pottery Co. began producing Loy-Nel-Art wares in 1905. The line's distinctive title came from the names of James McCoy's three sons, Lloyd, Nelson, and Arthur. Like other "standard" glazed pieces produced at this time by several Ohio potteries, Loy-Nel-Art has a glossy finish on a dark brown-black body, but Loy-Nel-Art featured a splash of green color on the front, and a burnt-orange splash on the back.

Three Loy-Nel-Art vases in different shapes, all unmarked. 8" tall 11 1/2" and 12" tall

$175-$225
$225-$275

Loy-Nel-Art jardinière, unmarked, 10" tall. **$275-$325**

Loy-Nel-Art Greek Key vase with roses, marked Loy-Nel-Art McCoy, 10" tall. **$275-$325**

Two Loy-Nel-Art vases, one with pansies and one with cherries, both marked Loy-Nel-Art McCoy, 6 1/2" tall. **$200-$275 each**

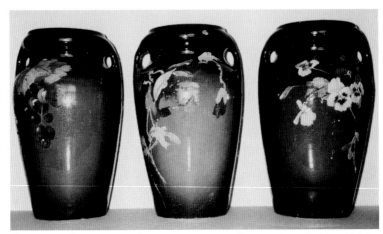

Three Loy-Nel-Art vases, with pansies, grapes, and roses, all marked Loy-Nel-Art McCoy, and two also marked "02", 13" tall.   **$425-$500 each**

Loy-Nel-Art vase, unmarked, 7" tall.
$175-$225

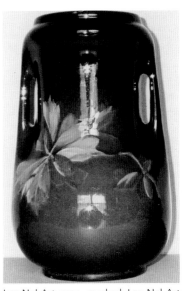

Loy-Nel-Art vase, marked Loy-Nel-Art McCoy, 10 1/2" tall.   **$375-$425**

Loy-Nel-Art jar with cigar decoration, unmarked, 4" by 4". **$250-$300**

Two Loy-Nel-Art vases with berries and flowers, both marked "03", 10 1/2" tall. **$325-$375 each**

Loy-Nel-Art vase with tulips, marked "03", 10 1/2" tall. **$325-$375**

Above: Loy-Nel-Art low footed bowl, marked "205-8," 4" by 8 1/2". **$175-$225**

Below: Non-production Loy-Nel-Art footed jardinière, un-marked, 11" by 12".
$750-$825

Two Loy-Nel-Art footed jardinières, one with cherries, one with flowers, both marked Loy-Nel-Art McCoy, 5" by 5 1/2". **$200-$275 each**

Three Loy-Nel-Art footed jardinières with floral decoration, all marked Loy-Nel-Art McCoy, 4 1/2" tall. **$175-$250 each**

Loy-Nel-Art vase with grapes, unmarked, 12 1/2" tall. **$475-$550**

Loy-Nel-Art vase with roses, marked Loy-Nel-Art McCoy, 15" tall. **$675-$750**

Loy-Nel-Art vase with flowers on the front and raised Indian motif on reverse, unmarked, 12" tall. **$525-$575 each**

Loy-Nel-Art pitcher, un-marked, 5 1/2" tall.
$200-$250

Loy-Nel-Art cuspidor with pansies, marked "206", 8" tall.   **$200-$250**

Two Loy-Nel-Art footed jardinières with flowers, marked Loy-Nel-Art McCoy, 8" and 7" tall.   **$325-$400 each**

Loy-Nel-Art jardinière and pedestal, unmarked; jardinière, 10" tall; pedestal 18" tall. **$675-$750/pair**

Loy-Nel-Art jardinière and pedestal, unmarked; jardinière, 8" tall; pedestal 18" tall. **$675-$750/pair**

Loy-Nel-Art jardinière and pedestal; jardinière, marked Loy-Nel-Art Mc-Coy 205, 9 1/2" tall; pedestal, marked 2050, 16 1/2" tall. **$1,200-$1,400/pair**

Loy-Nel-Art umbrella stand, marked Loy-Nel-Art McCoy, 21 1/2" tall. **$950-$1,100**

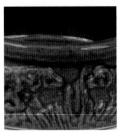

Pet Feeders

Some forms of McCoy pet feeders are being reproduced, and some potteries are still making dishes in vintage styles. So look for age signs like glaze crazing, discolored bases that may have an unglazed—or "dry"—foot ring, and compare weights, since old pieces are almost always heavier than later versions.

No. 4—7½" Dog Feeder
Green and Brown Lettering
To Man's Best Friend, His Dog
Packed 2 Doz. Wt. 55 lbs.
$9.70 per Dozen

No. 5—6" Spaniel Feeder
Green and Yellow
Packed 2 Doz. Wt. 47 lbs.
$9.70 per Dozen

A dog feeder and a spaniel feeder were included in a 1958 McCoy catalog.

Though sometimes called pet feeders, these three Stoneware dishes with Parading Elephants are also known as bulb bowls, 1920s. They have an unglazed or "dry" rim, and come with two bases, low (McCoy shield mark 87) and raised with a fluted border and tripod feet (Brush McCoy, unmarked).

Green is the most common glaze **$60-$70**
Blue **$80-$90**
Yellow **$100+**

Two versions of the Hunting Dog feeder with raised dog pattern, one with a dry rim and one glazed, 1930s, unmarked, 6 1/2" diameter.
$75-$90 each

Left: New dog dish (dogs running to right, lighter weight, brighter glaze). Right: Slightly different Bird Dog dish in green glaze, 7 1/2" diameter. **$75-$90**

Two sizes of dog dishes, with decals, 1970s, McCoy Mt. Clemens mark, 7" and 6 3/4" diameter.
$90-$110 each

Four "To Man's Best Friend, His Dog" bowls showing glaze and mold variations (dry rim is earlier), 1930s and '40s, McCoy Made in USA mark, 7 1/2" diameter. **$75-$90**

Left: Two "To Man's Best Friend, His Dog" bowls showing bottom mark. Right: Reproduction bowl, 6" diameter.

Cat and Dog feeders, 1940s, McCoy mark, 6" diameter.   **$75-$90 each**

Three "Dog. (Period)" bowls, also called Spaniel feeders because the tapered design kept the dog's ears out of the bowl, 1940s, McCoy mark or unmarked, 6 1/2" diameter.   **$75-$90 each**

Dog feeder, 1940s, glazed bottom, unmarked, 5" diameter.   **$50-$60**

Pet feeder, UNIPET treat bowl with bell in lid, late 1960s, UNIPET Upjohn mark.   **$45-$55**

Planters

Many collectors believe that planters represent the most varied and entertaining area of McCoy wares. From the simple leaf forms to the elaborate figural pieces featuring birds and animals, look for examples with crisp molds and good cold-paint or gilt trim. Check closely for damage or signs of restoration, especially on planters with applied birds and flowers.

Hanging planters were the theme of this spread in a 1976 McCoy catalog.

SILHOUETTE

Satin Glazed Planters

Our Golden Anniversary line featuring new shapes in satin glazes of white, green, turquoise, yellow, and brown. Available in a 22K brushed gold decoration or plain finish.

G1104 - 12"

G1101 - 6" 1107 - 6½" 1104 - 12"

G1108 - 8" 1103 - 10¼" 1101 - 6"

G1107 - 6½" G1103 - 10¼" G1106 - 7"

1109B - 10" 1106 - 7" 1108 - 8" 1105 - 7½" G1105 - 7½"

THE NELSON McCOY POTTERY COMPANY
Factory - Office   Roseville, Ohio

The Silhouette line of satin glazed planters came out when McCoy was celebrating its Golden Anniversary.

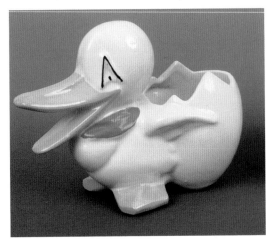

Bird planting dish, 1950s, McCoy mark, 10" wide. **$25-$35**

Duck and Egg planter with cold paint, 1950s, McCoy Made in USA mark, 3 1/2" tall.
$35-$45

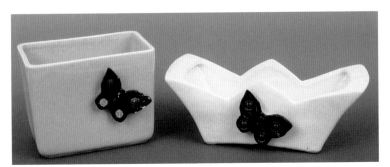

Two Jewel Line planters with applied butterflies, 1950s, McCoy USA mark.
$110-$125 each

Above left: Round planting dish, McCoy mark, 7" diameter. **$25-$35**
Above right: Window box, McCoy USA mark, 8 1/2" long. **$35-$45**

Leaves and Berries planter with hand-painted decoration under glaze, 1950s, McCoy USA mark, 5" tall.
$45-$55

Left: Rocking chair planter, with cold paint, 1950s, McCoy USA mark, 8 1/2" tall. **$50-$60**
Right: Chinaman planter, 1950s, McCoy USA mark, 5 1/2" tall. **$25-$30**

Floraline rock planter, 1960s, marked "Floraline 553 Lancaster USA," 8 1/2" long. **$45-$55**

Two Antelope window boxes (also called ferneries) in matte white and aqua, 1940s, NM mark (hard to find) and unmarked, come with grooved rim and without, 9 1/2" long. White **$90-$110**
Aqua **$45-$55**

Three Floraline footed planters, 1960s, style numbers 434 and T-519, all 7" diameter.
$12-$18 each

Two Antique Rose pieces in blue with transfer decoration: watering can and swan planter, each 7" tall, 1959, McCoy USA mark. **$45-$60 each**
Also found in white with red or brown rose.

Antelope planter, 1950s, unmarked, 12" long. **$400-$450**

Two Butterfly Line trough planters or window boxes in matte aqua and blue, 1940s, NM USA mark, 8 1/4" long. **$65-$75 each**

Two Butterfly Line hanging basket planters in matte blue and aqua, 1940s, NM mark, found with and without holes, 6 1/2" diameter. **$200-$225 each**

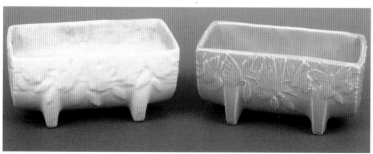

Two Butterfly Line trough planters, 1940s, NM USA mark, 5 1/2" long. **$35-$45 each**

Butterfly Line window box in matte aqua, 1940s, unmarked, hard to find this size, 9 1/4" long.
$150-$175
Marked, **$250**

Two Butterfly Line planters in matte aqua.
Left: Unmarked butterfly, 1940s, 7 1/2" wide.
Right: Ivy planter, 1940s, USA mark, 4" tall.

$125-$150
$65-$75

Flying ducks planter in natural colors, 1950s, McCoy USA mark, 10" wide. **$175-$225**

Flying ducks planter in raspberry and chartreuse, 1950s, McCoy USA mark, 10" wide. **$175-$225**

Two garden dishes or window boxes in matte blue and aqua, early 1940s, NM USA mark, rare, 9 1/4" long. **$110-$125**

Two trough planters or window boxes in matte aqua and blue, 1940s, NM USA mark, 7" long. **$45-$55 each**

Bird dog planter, 1950s, McCoy USA mark, also found in chartreuse with a black or brown dog, 8 1/2" tall. **$175-$225**

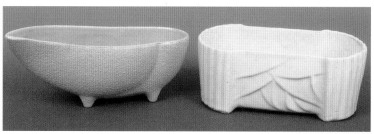

Two planters. Left: 1950s, McCoy USA mark, 9" long.
Right: 1940s, McCoy USA mark, 8 1/4" long.

$25-$35
$55-$65

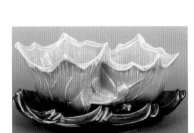

Humming Bird planter in blue, late 1940s, McCoy USA mark, 10 1/2" wide.
$125-$150

Humming Bird planter in green, late 1940s, McCoy USA mark, 10 1/2" wide.
$125-$150

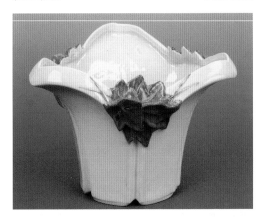

Three-sided ivy planter, 1950s, McCoy USA mark, hard to find, 6" tall.
$400-$500

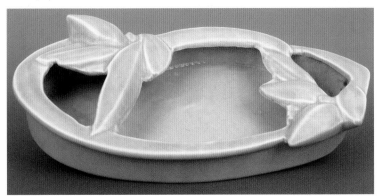

Lily Bud divided planting dish in matte aqua, 1940s, NM USA mark, 11 1/2" long.
$85-$95

Two Lily Bud planting dishes in matte aqua, 1940s, NM USA mark. Left: 9" long **$65-$75** Right: 8" long (called the cross) **$65-$75**

Left: Lily Bud "twig" planter in matte aqua, 1940s, NM USA mark, 5" tall. **$90-$110** Right: Lily Bud "banana boat" planter in matte aqua, NM USA mark, 8 1/2" long. **$55-$65**

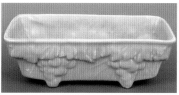

Grapes window box in matte aqua (rare), 1940s, NM USA mark, 10" long. **$110-$125**

Low planting dish with drape design in matte aqua, 1940s, NM USA mark, 8 1/2" diameter. **$65-$75** (rarely found without inverted lip)

Two window boxes in matte aqua and blue, 1940s, NM USA, 8 1/4" long. **$65-$75**

Two Sand Butterfly trough planters in matte aqua and glossy coral, 1930s, USA mark, 8 3/4" long. Matte colors **$50-$65** Coral **$65+**

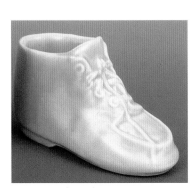

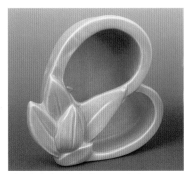

Mary Jane shoe planter in matte aqua, 1940s, NM USA mark. **$35-$45**

Lily Bud divided planting dish in matte blue, 1940s, NM USA mark, 6 1/2" wide. **$65-$75**

Left: Strawberry planter in matte blue, stoneware, 1930s, unmarked, 6 1/2" tall. **$85-$95**

Right: Shell planter in matte aqua, also found in glossy colors, 1940s NM USA mark, 7 1/2" long. **$55-$65**

Left: Baby Crib planter, part of the Nursery Line, 1950s, unmarked, 6 1/2" long. **$30-$40**
Right: Hanging Strawberry planter, 1950s, McCoy USA mark, 6" tall. **$50-$60**

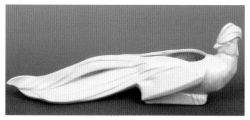

Bird of Paradise planter in glossy white (rarely found with cold-paint details), 1940s, McCoy mark, 13" long.
$55-$65

Swan planter in matte aqua, 1940s, unmarked, 5" tall. **$45-$55**

Left: Cornucopia planter with tassels in matte yellow, 1940s, McCoy mark, 8" tall. **$55-$65**
Right: Hanging basket planter, stoneware, 1930s, unmarked, 7" diameter. **$85-$95**

Left: Panda and Cradle planter, 1940s, McCoy USA mark, some pandas and blankets are cold painted, 5 1/2" tall. **$110-$125**
Right: Bonnet Duck and Egg planter, 1940s, McCoy mark, cold paint, 5 3/4" tall. **$175-$225**

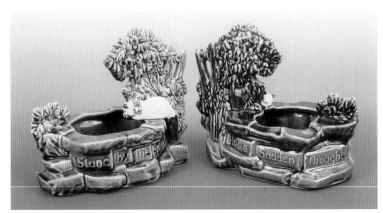

Two Pussy at the Well planters, 1950s, McCoy USA mark, 7" tall. **$125-$150 each**

Single cache planter in black and pink, 1950s, McCoy USA mark, 9" wide.
$70-$80

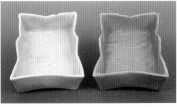

Two planting dishes in matte pink and aqua, 1940s, NM USA mark, 9" long.
$35-$40 each

Three figural planters in glossy aqua.
Left: Singing Bird, 1940s, unmarked, found in other colors, 4 1/2" tall. **$30-$40**
Center: Parrot, 1940s, NM USA mark, also found in pink and white, 7" tall. **$40-$50**
Right: Backwards Bird, 1940s, NM USA mark, also found in white and yellow, 4 1/2" tall.
$60-$70

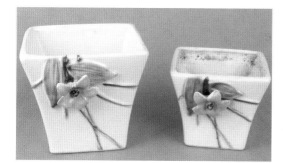

Blossomtime planters in matte white, 1940s, McCoy mark, (also found in yellow), 6" and 5" tall.
$50-$75 each

Singing Bird planter in matte white, 1940s, USA mark, found in other colors, 4 1/2" tall. **$30-$40**
(also found in 6 3/4" size)

Strawberry planter in matte white, stone-ware, 1930s, unmarked, 6 1/2" tall.
$60-$70

Two versions of the Rabbit planter, yellow version never had cold paint, 1950s, McCoy mark, 7 1/4" tall. **$100-$150 each**, depending on paint condition.

Log planter with gold trim, 1950s, McCoy mark, also found in green, 12 1/2" long
$110-$125 with gold trim
$80-$90 without gold trim

Two Snowman plant-
ers with cold-painted
details, late 1940s,
McCoy mark, 6" tall.
$70-$90 each
(depending on paint
condition)

Petal basket planter, 1950s, McCoy USA mark, 8 3/4" tall. **$150-$175**

Pine cone planter, mid-1940s, McCoy USA mark, 8" wide, rare. **$500-$600**
(A slightly larger planter in rust glaze, **$1,800-$2,000**)

Turtle planter with lily pad in atypical glaze (often found with yellow cold-paint decoration), early 1950s, McCoy mark, 8" long. Normally **$60-$70**
As shown **$150-$200**

Village Smithy planter in atypical burgundy and gray (usually in brown and green), 1950s, McCoy USA mark.
As shown **$300-$350**
In common glaze **$70-$80**

Two hanging basket planters, in brown and green and matte white, 1930s, unmarked, 6" diameter. **$70-$90 each**

Left: Scoop planter in forest green, late 1950s, McCoy mark, 6" wide. **$25-$35**
Right: low Vine planter with under-glaze decoration, mid-1950s, McCoy mark, 8 1/2" wide. **$35-$45**

Square textured planters in glossy green, interlocking, 1950s, unmarked, 3 1/2" and 5" tall. **$25-$30 each**

Two forms of Strawberry planters, one in atypical dusty burgundy, one in glossy green, stoneware, 1930s, unmarked, 7" tall. **$60-$70 each**
(This form is also found with a raised leaf motif on the body, called style #2.)

Large Turtle planter, 1950s, McCoy mark, 12 1/2" long.   **$125-$150**
(also found in other color combinations)

Snail planter, 1960s, Floraline mark.
                                    $40-$50

Two Harmony boat planters, early 1960s, McCoy mark, also found in orange and a brighter yellow, 8 1/2" and 9 1/2" long.   **$25-$30 each**

Left: Harmony boat planter in gold trim, 1960s, McCoy USA mark, 12" long. **$40-$50**
Right: Crestwood footed planter, 1960s, McCoy USA mark, 4 1/2" tall.   **$40-$50**

Small Hobnail planter in matte aqua, early 1940s, unmarked, probably a cut-down vase, 3 1/4" tall. **No established value.**

Left: square-top Hobnail planter in matte aqua, 1940s, NM USA mark, 4" tall. **$55-$65**

Right: Ball planter in glossy aqua (also called rose bowl), 1940s, NM USA mark, 3 1/2" tall. **$45-$55**

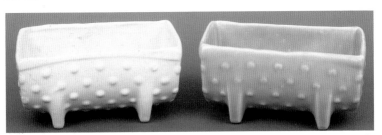

Two Hobnail trough planters in matte white and aqua, 1940s, NM USA mark, 5 1/2" long. **$30-$40 each**

Two Hobnail trough planters in matte blue and aqua, 1940s, NM USA mark, 8 1/2" long. **$50-$60 each**

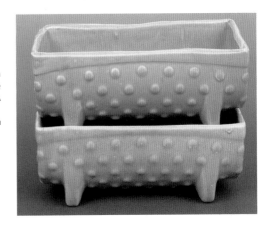

Caterpillar planter, 1960s, Floraline mark, 13 1/2" long, also found in brown, white, and yellow. **$40-$50**

Turtle planter, 1960s, Floraline mark. **$40-$50**

Two Floraline planters—bear and turtle—in glossy brown glaze, 1960s, Floraline mark (may also be marked USA or McCoy), each 3 1/2" tall. **$15-$20 each**

Three animal planters—kitten, puppy, and fawn—in pearly gray and rustic brown (glazes may vary), 1970s, marks include McCoy USA LCC and USA, with serial numbers 3026, 3027, and 3028, 6 3/4" to 7 1/2" tall. **$75-$90 each**

Three fruit planters—all oranges in varying glazes—1950s, McCoy USA mark, all 6 1/2" long. **$70-$90 each**

Three fruit planters—apple, pear, and grapes— 1950s, McCoy USA mark, all 6 1/2" long.
Apple and pear   **$60-$70 each**
Grapes   **$150-$175**

Bottom of fruit planter showing McCoy USA mark and employee letter stamp, "U."

Three fruit planters—lemon, banana, and pomegranate—1950s, McCoy USA mark; all 6 1/2" long. Lemon and banana   **$100-$125 each**
Pomegranate   **$125-$150**

Left: Mammy on Scoop planter (also found with yellow scoop), cold-paint decoration, 1950s, McCoy mark, 7 1/2" long. **$175-$200**

Right: Boy on Rolling Pin planter (also found with yellow pin), cold-paint decoration, 1950s, McCoy mark, 7 1/2" long. **$125-$150**

Frog with Umbrella and Duck with Umbrella planters, mid-1950s, McCoy mark, with cold-paint decoration, 7 1/2" tall. **$150-$200 each**

Left: Calypso Line barrel planter, late 1950s, McCoy mark, with cold-paint decoration, 5" tall. **$125-$150** depending on paint condition

Right: Donkey with Bananas planter, 1950s, only one known to exist, 6" tall. **$1,500+**

Calypso Line Banana Boat planter, with cold-paint decoration (also found with all under-glaze color), late 1950s, McCoy mark, 11" long. **$175-$200**

Wash Tub Woman planter, not a production piece but marked NM, 6" tall, ex-Cope Collection, with damage. **$1,000**

Pair of ribbed and footed planters in matte white, late 1940s, unmarked, 6" tall (also come in 8" size). **$70-$80/pair**

Three animal planters (cat with a bow, kittens with a basket, and puppy with turtle) in gold trim, 1950s, McCoy mark; kitten 7" tall.　　　　**$70-$80 each**

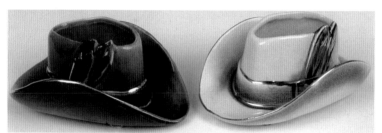

Hat planters in brown and beige with gold trim, 1950s, McCoy USA and Shafer marks, 8" long.　　　　**$60-$75 each**

Left: Liberty Bell planter with gold trim, with 8th of July error (later corrected to 4th of July, rare), 1950s, McCoy USA mark, 8 1/4" tall.　　　　**$300-$350**
Right: Quail planter in gold trim, 1950s, McCoy USA and Shafer mark, 7" tall.　　　　**$125-$150**

Liberty Bell planter with correct date and black bell in cold paint.
$350-$400
(depending on paint condition)

Left: Alligator planter in gold trim, 1950s, McCoy USA, 10" long.　　**$125-$150**
Right: Pedestal planter in gold trim, 1950s, McCoy mark.　　**$90-$110**

Left: Village Smithy planter in gold trim, 1950s, McCoy USA mark, 6 1/2" tall.
Right: Spinning wheel planter with cat and dog, 1950s, McCoy mark, 7 1/4" tall.
$90-$110 each

Left: Kittens with basket planter in gold trim in another glaze combination, 1950s, McCoy mark, 7" tall.
$70-$80
Right: Grapes planter in gold trim (rare), 1940s to '50s, McCoy USA mark, 6 1/2" long. **$275-$325**

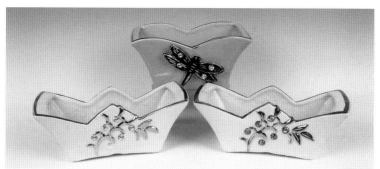

Three Jeweled Line planters in gold trim, 1950s, McCoy USA and Shafer marks, one with dragonfly, decorated with rhinestones (often missing), 7 1/2" and 8 1/2" wide.
Dragonfly **$150-$200**
Others **$90-$110 each**

Left: Short Scroll planter, 1950s, USA and Shafer marks, 4 1/2" tall. **$50-$60**
Right: Swan planter in Sunburst glaze, 1950s, "USA McCoy 192 24K Gold" mark, also with atypical pink interior, 4 1/2" tall. **$100-$125**

Triple Pot planter in gold trim, 1950s, McCoy USA mark, 12 1/2" long. **$200-$225**

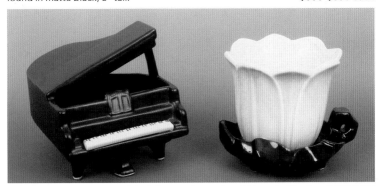

Two Piano planters in gold trim in white and yellow, late 1950s, McCoy USA mark, also found in matte black, 5" tall. **$300-$350 each**

Left: Piano planter in matte black, late 1950s, McCoy USA mark, 5" tall. **$150-$175**
Right: Tulip planter in pink and black, 1950s, McCoy USA mark, also found in green and gray, 4 1/2" tall. **$60-$70**

Left: Small fin planter, early 1950s, USA McCoy mark, 3 1/2" tall. **$50-$60**
Right: Trinket box in unusual brocade glaze, 1960s, McCoy USA 464 mark,3 1/2" tall.
$70-$80

Two planters in gold trim. Left: Rooster on Wheelbarrow, mid-1950s, McCoy USA and Shafer marks, 7" tall. **$200-$225**
Right: Lamb with Bells, mid-1950s, McCoy mark, rare in gray, 7 1/2" tall. **$100-$125**

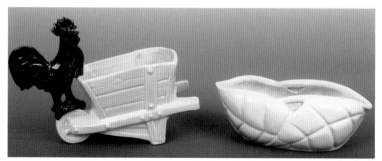

Left: Rooster on Wheelbarrow planter in black and yellow (rare colors), mid-1950s, McCoy USA mark, 7" tall. **$150-$170 in these colors**
Right: Leaf planter, 1940s, McCoy mark, 9" long. **$50-$70**

Left: Lotus leaf planter in gold trim, 1950s, McCoy USA mark, 4 1/2" tall. **$50-$60**
Right: Water Lily planter, 1950s, McCoy USA mark, also found in green and rarely in orange, 3 1/2" tall. **$100-$125**

Triple Fawn planter in gold trim, 1950s, McCoy USA mark, 12" wide. **$400-$450** (Same price range for black and chartreuse glaze.)

Triple Fawn planter in natural colors. **$250-$275**

Two small Log planters in gold trim, 1950s, McCoy and McCoy USA marks, 7" and 8 3/4" long. **$35-$45 each**

Left: Sand Butterfly planter (also called a fern box) in gold trim, 1940s, McCoy USA mark, found in other pearly colors, 8 1/2" long. **$45-$55**
Right: Scallop-edge planter in gold trim, early 1960s, McCoy USA mark, 9" long. **$35-$45**

Left: Ball planter in gold trim (also called rose bowl), 1940s, NM USA mark, 3 1/2" tall. **$45-$55**
This form also comes in a 7" tall size with a McCoy mark. **$70-$80** in gold trim

Left: Basket planter in gold trim, 1950s, McCoy USA and Shafer mark, 9" wide. **$75-$90**
Right: Lotus form planter (also called Brown Drip centerpiece) in gold trim, 1950s, McCoy mark, 9" wide. **$45-$55**

Left: Centerpiece bowl/planter with applied bird in gold trim, 1950s, McCoy mark, 10" wide. **$60-$75**

Right: Frog and Lotus planter, late 1940s, unmarked, 4" tall. **$35-$45**

(Beware of reproductions.)

Two Stork planters in gold trim, part of the Nursery Line, 1950s, McCoy USA and Shafer marks, rare in yellow, 7" tall. **$110-$125 each**

Two Rocking Horse planters, one in gold trim, one plain yellow (rare), part of the Nursery Line, 1950s, McCoy USA and Shafer mark. Gold trim **$200-$225**

Yellow **$225-$250**

Pink or green **$125-$150**

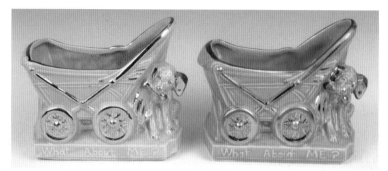

Two Baby Buggy planters (called "What About Me?") in gold trim, part of the Nursery Line, 1950s, McCoy USA mark, 6" tall. **$125-$150 each**
(without gold trim **$70-$80**)

Two Cradle planters, one in gold trim, one plain, part of the Nursery Line, 1950s McCoy mark, 8 1/2" long. With gold trim **$70-$80**
Plain **$45-$55**

Two Nursery Line planters. Left: Dog with Cart, 1950s, McCoy USA mark,8 1/2" long.
$45-$55
Right: Lamb with Bow, 1950s, McCoy USA mark, with cold paint, 8 1/2" long.
$45-$55, depending on paint condition

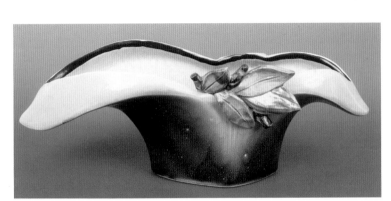

Fancy Lily Bud planting dish, late 1940s or early 50s, hand-painted under glaze, 11" long. **$85-$95**

Planter with stand, 1950s, McCoy USA mark, 7" long. **$35-$45** (with stand, which is often missing)

Triple bulb bowl in pink and black, 1950s, McCoy mark, 8" wide. **$165-$185**

Left: Lotus planter in gold trim, 1950s, McCoy USA mark, 4 1/2" tall. **$50-$60**
Right: Swimming duck planter in gold trim, 1950s, McCoy USA mark. **$70-$80**

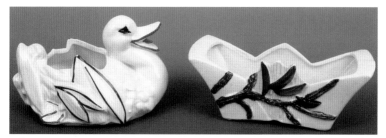

Left: Swimming duck planter with cold paint, 1950s, McCoy USA mark, 7" long.
$45-$55
Right: Vine design planting dish with hand-painted decoration under glaze, 1950s, McCoy USA mark, 8 1/2" long.
$60-$70

Left: planter, came with metal stand, 1950s, McCoy USA mark. **$25-$35** with stand
Right: planting dish, 1940s, McCoy mark. **$35-$45**

Left: Double Cornucopia planter in gold trim, 1960s, McCoy may be visible depending on glaze thickness. **$25-$30**
Right: Cup planter with gold decoration, 1970s, McCoy LCC mark. **$10**

Left: Stork planter in green, part of the Nursery Line, 1950s, McCoy USA mark, 7" tall. **$110-$125**
Right: Snooty Poodle planter (pierced base), 1950s, McCoy USA mark, also found in green and commonly in black, 7" tall. **$75-$90**

Four Nursery Line planters, all came with cold-paint decoration, 1950s, unmarked. Prices vary depending on paint condition.
Lamb with block, 4 1/2" tall. **$55-$65**
Baby scale, 5 1/2" tall. **$35-$45**
Rattle, 5 1/2" long. **$70-$80**
Raggedy Ann and blocks, 5 1/2" tall. **$75-$85**

Left: Snooty Poodle planter (closed base, harder to find) in black with cold paint Mc-Coy USA mark, 7" tall.   **$90-$110**
Right: Clown Riding a Pig planter with cold paint, early 1950s, McCoy USA mark 8 1/2" long.   **$110-$125**
(Also found with pig having raised ears, rare.)

Two Cat with Basket planters in glossy pink and yellow, early 1940s, NM USA mark, also found in white, 6" tall. **$50-$60 each**

Left: Frog with Umbrella planter in black (rare), mid-1950s, McCoy USA mark, with cold-paint decoration, 7 1/2" tall. **$150-$200**
Right: Carriage with Umbrella, mid-1950s, McCoy USA mark, 9" tall. **$150-$200**

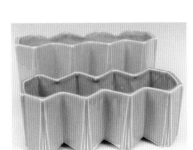

Two jagged edge planters, 1950s, Mc-Coy USA mark, also found in yellow, 10" long. **$150-$200 each**

Large Fish planter in pink, green and white, 1950s, McCoy USA mark, 12" long. **$1,200+**

Left: Boot and Football planter in a non-production glaze, normally found in all brown with white or yellow cold paint, 1950s, McCoy USA mark, 4 1/4" tall. **$400-$450** as shown, normally **$125-$175**

Right: Fence and Birds pot and saucer, non-production piece, 1950s, McCoy USA mark, 4 1/2" tall. **$200-$250**

Three Stretch Animal planters (horse, butting goat, small lion), late 1930s to early '40s, unmarked, 3 1/4" to 4" tall.

Horse	**$75-$90**
Goat	**$250-$300**
Lion	**$250-$300**

(There are also a standing goat, dachshund, angry dog, and larger lion in the Stretch Animals.)

Small Stretch Lion in rare cobalt blue, 1940s, unmarked, 4" tall. **$250-$300**

Baa Baa Black Sheep planter, part of the Nursery Line, 1930s, NM USA mark, also found in yellow, blue, and white.
$50-$60

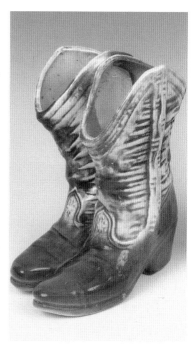

Cowboy boots planter (this form also used for lamp base), 1960s, McCoy USA mark, 7" tall. **$75-$85**

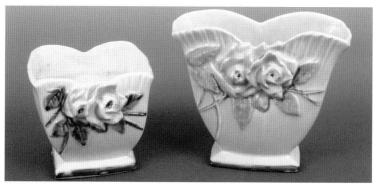

Two Wild Rose planters in matte lavender and aqua, 1950s, McCoy mark.
4 1/2" tall **$40-$45**
6" tall **$50-$60**

Two Wild Rose planters in matte yellow, 1950s, McCoy mark. 8 1/4" wide. **$60-$75**
6" tall **$45-$55**

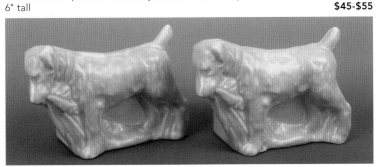

Two Dog with Blanket planters (it's actually an Airedale holding a coat in its mouth, but nobody calls it that) in aqua and lavender, 1940s, NM USA mark, 5" tall. **$90-$110 each**

Two Stretch Animal planters, dachshund and large lion, in matte aqua, 1930s, unmarked. Dachshund, 8 1/2" long **$150-$175**
Lion, 5 1/2" tall **$350-$400**

Two Lion planters in matte aqua and "butterfly blue," 1940s, NM USA mark, also found in yellow and white, 8 1/4" long. **$110-$125 each**

Two Nursery Line planters. Left: Rabbits and Stump in yellow and blue (rare), also found in brown and yellow, and rustic ivory and brown, 1950s, McCoy USA mark as shown. **$150-$175**
Right: Lamb with Two Bells planter in rare gray, 1950s, McCoy mark, 7 1/2" tall. **$125-$150**

Two figural planters in matte aqua. Left: Rooster, 1940s, NM mark, 6" tall. **$60-$70**
Right: Pelican, 1940s, NM mark, 7 1/2" long. **$45-$50**

Swan planting dish in rustic ivory and turquoise, 1950s, McCoy USA mark, 8 1/2" tall. **$700-$800**

Swan planting dish in chartreuse and black, 1950s, McCoy USA mark, 8 1/2" tall. **$700-$800**

Two Pony planters in matte aqua and yellow, 1940s, NM USA mark, 5" tall. **$80-$90 each**

Two Deer planters in matte aqua. Left: Doe and fawn, 1940s, NM USA mark or unmarked (reissued in the 1950s in glossy yellow and green), 7" tall. **$60-$70**
Right: Backwards deer (one of the "ladder pieces," so named because they were pictured in an early McCoy guide on a drying rack that was tiered like the steps of a ladder), 1940s, NM mark, 4 1/2" tall. **$80-$90**

Left: Stump planter with rare "Ted & Anne" theme, 1950s, McCoy mark, also found in yellow and green, 4" tall. **$60-$70**

Right: Swans planter in green, 1950s, McCoy mark, common in white and yellow, 8 1/2" long. In green **$30-$40**

Left: Stump planter with more common "ST-VH" initials in glossy brown, 1950s, McCoy mark, also found in yellow and green, 4" tall. **$25-$35**

Right: Ducks and eggs planter in purple glaze (rare color), 1950s, McCoy USA mark, 5" tall. **$55-$65** in this color, otherwise **$30-$40**

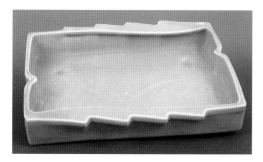

Zigzag planting dish in matte aqua, 1940s, NM USA mark, 9 1/2" long. **$110-$125**

Two Petal basket planters (uncommon in darker glazes at left), 1950s, McCoy USA mark, 8 3/4" tall.
Darker   **$110-$125**
Lighter   **$75-$90**

Left: Swimming Swan planter with under-glaze decoration, 1950s, McCoy mark, 7" tall.   **$40-$50**
Right: Harmony planting dish, 1960s, McCoy USA mark, 8 1/2" long.   **$20-$25**

Left: Pheasant planter, 1950s, McCoy USA mark, 6" tall.   **$70-$80**
Right: Puppy planter, late 1950s, McCoy USA mark, 6" tall.   **$50-$60**

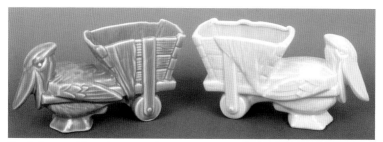

Two Pelican and Cart planters in glossy aqua and yellow, 1940s, NM mark, 4 1/2" tall.
$55-$65 each

Two Cornucopia planters in glossy aqua and yellow, 1940s, NM USA mark, also found in white, 5" tall.
$30-$35 each

Two "S" planting dishes in matte white (tripod feet) and glossy aqua (four curving line feet), 1940s, NM USA mark, note that white dish is slightly shallower, 8" long.
$25-$30 each

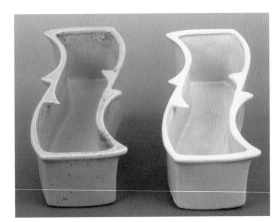

Two Spiked planters in matte aqua and pink, 1950s, McCoy USA mark, 9" long.
$50-$60 each

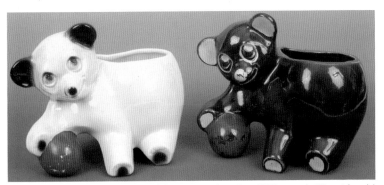

Two Bear and Ball planters, part of the Nursery line, late 1940 or early 50s, with cold paint, McCoy USA mark, 5 1/2" tall. **$125-$150 each**

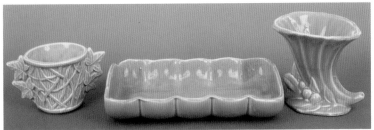

Left: Ivy planter, 1950s, McCoy USA mark, 3" tall. $30-$40
Center: Planting dish, 1940s, NM USA mark, 9" long. $35-$45
Right: Small Cornucopia planter, 1950s, unmarked, 4 1/2" tall. $35-$45

Round planting dish in matte aqua, late 1940s, McCoy mark, 8 1/4" diameter.
$35-$45

Two small Trough planters in glossy white and aqua, late 1950s, USA mark, 6" wide.
$20-$25 each

Two Bird Dog planters, late 1950s, McCoy USA mark, one with speckled glaze, 7 3/4" long.
$125-$150 each

Pedestal Line window box or planting dish, 1959, McCoy USA mark, 11" wide. **$35-$40**

Cat with Bow planter with cold paint decoration, 1950s, McCoy USA mark on back, 7" long.
$40-$50

Large Turtle planter in dark green and pink, 1950s, McCoy USA mark, 12 1/2" long. **$175-$225**

Window box in glossy pink, 1950s, McCoy mark, 10" wide. **$25-$30**

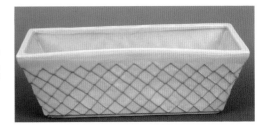

Elephant planter in matte aqua, attributed to McCoy, unmarked, 9" tall, with attribution. **$100**

Large Centerpiece planter, 1950s, McCoy USA mark, found in other colors, 12" long. **$90-$110**

Two Wishing Well planters, late 1940s to early '50s, McCoy USA mark, gray and turquoise glaze is harder to find. 6" tall **$25-$35**
Larger (7") size **$55-$65**

Two Lamb planters in glossy black and gray, 1940s, NM USA mark, 3" tall.
$55-$65 each

Auto planter, 1950s, unmarked, 6" tall.
$45-$55

Large Leaf planter in matte green, 1930s, stoneware, unmarked, 6 1/2" tall.
$80-$90
(This form was reissued in the 1950s as part of the Garden Club Line.)

Two Crestwood pieces. Left, Pedestal planter, 12" tall. Right, Boat planter, 13" long, mid-1960s, McCoy USA with original labels.
$60-$70 each

Grecian Line window box, 1950s, McCoy USA mark with style number 435, 12" long. **$85-$95**

Grecian Line pedestal planter, 1950s, McCoy USA mark with style number 442, 8" wide. **$50-$60**

Basket planter hand-painted by Leslie Cope, signed, 7" tall. **No established value.**

Rustic Line planter with seven wide-eyed animal faces (probably intended to be fawns) peering out of the foliage, called by some collectors "the devil dog planter" or "gremlins planter," 1940s, McCoy mark, 6" tall. **$60-$70**

Left: Icicles window box, 1950s, McCoy USA mark, 8 1/2" long. **$70-$80**
Right: Garden Club pedestal planter, late 1950s, McCoy USA mark, 7" tall. **$40-$50**

Two views of the Zebra planter, 1950s, McCoy USA mark, 8 1/2" long. **$800**

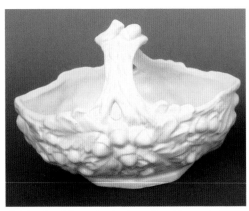

Oak Leaf and Acorn basket in matte white, early 1950s, McCoy USA mark. **$60-$70**

Parrot planter in matte white, 1940s, NM mark, 7 1/2" tall. **$70-$80**

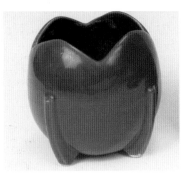

Ball planter (also called rose bowl), 1940s, NM mark. 3 1/2" tall. **$35-$45** (This form also comes in a 7" tall size with a McCoy mark, **$60-$70**.)
The shorter size was a popular choice for glaze tests and may be found with inscribed glaze numbers.

Small planter usually found in pink or blue, with under-glaze decoration, 1940s, 5" tall. **$45-$55**

Right: Water Lily planter with green and tan details, normally found in all green and yellow, 1950s, unmarked, 7 1/4" long. **$50-$60**

Old Mill planter, 1950s, McCoy USA mark, 6 1/2" tall. **$90-$110**

Large Fish planter, found in other colors, 1950s, McCoy mark, 12" long.
$1,200-$1,400

Small Cornucopia planter in gold trim, 1950s, McCoy mark, 4" tall. **$40-$50**

Leaves and Berries hanging basket planter in matte green, 1930s, unmarked, 5 1/4" diameter. **$60-$70**

Butterfly hanging basket planter in non-production dark green glaze, early 1940s, NM mark. As shown **$500-$600**
In pastel colors **$225-$250**

Leaves and Berries hanging basket planter in matte aqua, 1930s, unmarked, 6" tall. **$50-$60**

Signs

McCoy Pottery sign. intended for use at JC Penney stores, 4" by 5 1/4".
$400-$450

Block used to make the mold for "The Pottery Shop by McCoy" signs.　　**$1,000**

McCoy Pottery sign, contemporary, by Billie and Nelson McCoy, 4" by 5 1/4". **$250-$300**

McCoy Pottery sign, contemporary, by Billie and Nelson McCoy, signed and dated 2001, 4 1/2" by 8 1/2". **$40-$50**

Vases and Flower Holders

Second only to planters in their variety, vases also present special challenges, because many of them lack formal names. Collectors use descriptions like "the vase with the low drape handles" or "the one that looks like a chevron." Others define collecting areas based on glazes (matte aqua or the glossy palette) and seek examples in the smaller sizes.

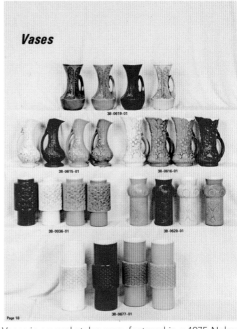

Vases in several styles were featured in a 1975 Nelson McCoy catalog.

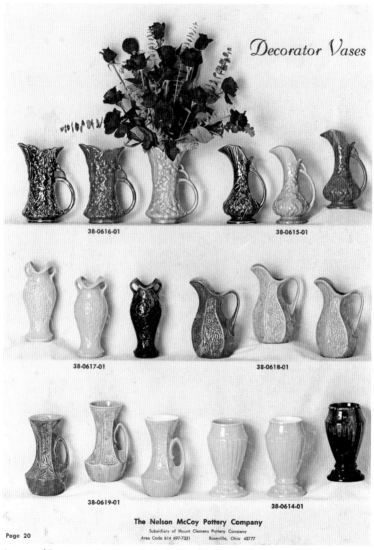

Decorator Vases

38-0616-01   38-0615-01

38-0617-01   38-0618-01

38-0619-01   38-0614-01

The Nelson McCoy Pottery Company
Subsidiary of Mount Clemens Pottery Company
Area Code 614 697-7331 Roseville, Ohio 43777

A page of Decorator Vases was included in a McCoy catalog.

Two Arrow Leaf vases in matte aqua and coral, 1940s, McCoy mark or unmarked, 7 1/2" tall.
$85-$95 each

Two Butterfly Line "V" vases in matte blue and yellow, 1940s, NM USA mark, 9" tall.   **$90-$110**

Three Butterfly Line vases in matte blue, yellow, and white. Left: cylinder vase, 1940s, NM USA or NM mark, 8" tall.   **$75-$85**
Center: Two-handledvase, 1940s, USA mark, 10" tall.
$200-$225
Right: Cylinder vase, NM mark, 6" tall.   **$55-$65**

Two Butterfly Line cylinder vases in matte white and yellow, 1940s, NM USA mark, 8" tall.
$75-$85 each

Two Antique Rose pieces in blue with transfer decoration. Flower bowl, 9 1/2" wide, and pitcher vase, 9" tall, 1959, McCoy USA mark. **$45-$55 each** Also found in white with red or brown rose.

Antique Rose low flower bowl in blue with transfer decoration, 1959, McCoy USA mark, 12" wide.
$55-$65
Also found in white with red or brown rose.

Vases and Flower Holders

Vase in glossy yellow (rare, sometimes called an Arrow Leaf but different from other vases in that form), 1950s, McCoy mark, 8" tall. **$550-$600**

Two vases in matte coral and aqua, one faceted, one smooth, 1940s, NM mark 9" tall. **$55-$65 each**

Tassel vase in glossy rasp-berry, 1930s, stoneware, unmarked, 8" tall.
$75-$85

Two vases in glossy coral and yellow, 1950s, McCoy mark, 9" tall. **$60-$70 each**

Two vases in glossy white, late 1950s, unmarked, 8 1/2" and 8 1/4" tall. Left, with transfer decoration of roses **$45-$55**
Right **$65-$75**

Two Hand vases in matte aqua, 1940s, NM USA mark.
7 1/2" tall **$125-$150**
5" tall **$55-$65**

Three small flower holders in glossy white, pink, and yellow, 1930s, NM mark or unmarked, 3 1/4" tall. **$60-$70 each**
McCoy matte colors include aqua, blue, lavender, white, yellow, and brown and green.

Leaves and Berries vase in matte brown and green, unmarked, 7" tall. **$80-$90**

Vase in matte brown and green, 12" tall. **$150-$175**

Pink Poppy vases showing variations in glaze intensity, McCoy mark, 8 1/2" wide. **$350-$450 each**

Heart vase in matte white, unmarked, 6" tall, and spherical Leaves and Berries vase, unmarked, 6 1/2" tall. **$60-$70 each**

Blossomtime vases in yellow, 1940s, McCoy mark, one matte, one glossy.
6 3/4" tall **$70-$80**
8" tall **$60-$70**

Blossomtime vases in matte white, 1940s, McCoy mark.
6 3/4" tall **$70-$80**
8" tall **$60-$70**

Two Blossomtime vases, 1940s, McCoy mark, 6 1/2" tall. **$50-$60 each**

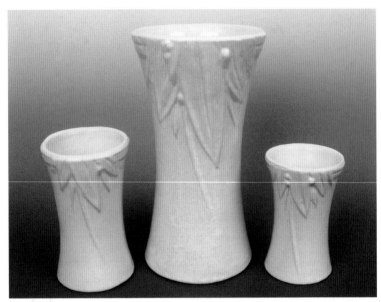

Three Stoneware Hourglass vases in matte white, 1930s, unmarked, also found in yellow, pink, varying shades of green, and brown and green.

12" tall	**$200-$225**
8" tall	**$90-$110**
6" tall	**$75-$90**

Grape pitcher vase in matte white, 9" tall, early 1950s, McCoy mark.
$50-$60

Two Hourglass vases in matte yellow and pink, 1930s, unmarked, 8" tall. **$90-$110 each**

Four Stoneware Hourglass vases in matte white, unmarked, 1930s, also found in varying shades of green, and brown and green.

5" tall	**$50-$60**
10" tall	**$100-$125**
14" tall	**$225-$250**

Left: Leaves and Berries Hourglass vase in matte green glaze, 1930s, stoneware, unmarked, 14" tall. **$400-$450**
Right: Stoneware Urn vase in glossy green glaze, hard-to-find form, 1930s, unmarked, 8" tall. **$250-$275**

Left: Cat vase in matte black (also found in white and gray), 1960s, McCoy USA, 14" tall. **$225-$250**
Right: Antique Curio Line vase in glossy brown (also found in green and white), 1960s, McCoy USA mark, 14 1/2" tall. **$110-$125**

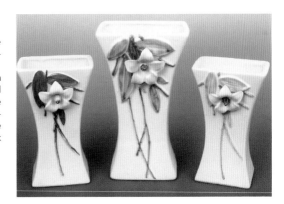

Three Blossomtime vases, mid-1940s, Mc-Coy mark.

$100-$150 each because of atypical flower and leaf glaze colors. Normally $50-$60 each in white or yellow with pink flowers.

Three Lily Bud vases in matte white and yellow, 1940s, NM USA mark (also found unmarked).

8" tall **$80-$90 each**

10" tall **$125-$150 each**

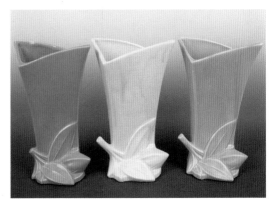

Three Lily Bud vases in matte blue, lavender, and aqua, 1940s, NM USA mark (also found unmarked). 10" tall.

$125-$150 each (Note short stem on blue vase, not a break, as it came from the factory.)

Three tall Cornucopia vases in matte white, 1930s, unmarked.
5" tall $75-$100
8" tall $50-$75
10" tall $100-$125

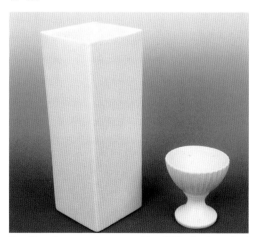

Two Floraline vases in matte white, 1960s, both marked
Floraline USA. 10" rectangular vase **$45-$55**
3 1/2" chalice **$15-$20**

Square Cherry vase, stoneware, 1930s, unmarked. **$100-$125**

Left: Leafy vase in matte white, 1940s, unmarked, 7 1/2" tall. **$100-$125**
Center and right: Two Arrow Leaf vases in matte white, 1940s, unmarked.
10" tall **$125-$150**
8" tall **$90-$110**

Ram's Head vase in matte white (rare, usually chartreuse, black, or burgundy), 1950s, McCoy mark, 9 1/2" tall. **$250-$300**
(in other colors, **$100-$125**)

Large Fan vase, also called "Blades of Grass," glossy white (also found in green and black), late 1950s, McCoy USA mark, 10" tall. **$175-$225**

Two Baluster vases in matte white, 1940s, unmarked, heights vary from 12" to almost 13". With handles **$150-$175** Without handles **$200-$250**

Left: Fin or Ribbed vase in matte white, 14" tall, unmarked. **$250-$300**
Right: Fin or Ribbed planter in matte white, 7" tall, unmarked (may also be found with saucer base). **$90-$110**

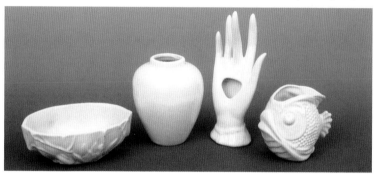

From left: Lily Bud pin dish, NM mark, 5 1/2" wide. **$40-$50**
Miniature oil jar, 4 1/4" tall. **$40-$50**
Small Hand vase (fingers separated), 6 1/2" tall. **$100-$125**
Fish flower holder (one of the "ladder pieces," so named because they were pictured in an early McCoy guide on a drying rack that was tiered like the steps of a ladder), 1940s to 1950s, 3 1/4" tall. **$90-$125**, depending on color

Three Fish flower holders (one of the "ladder pieces," so named because they were pictured in an early McCoy guide on a drying rack that was tiered like the steps of a ladder), 1940s, NM USA mark, 3 1/4" tall. **$90-$125**, depending on color

Miniature Turtle flower holder (one of the "ladder pieces," so named because they were pictured in a early McCoy guide on a drying rack that was tiered like the steps of a ladder), 1940s to 1950s, NM mark, 4" long. **$80-$100**

Miniature Vase flower holder, NM mark, 3" tall.
$55-$65

Two matte white vases, one with leaves (Stoneware, late 1920s), one with loop handles, 1930s, unmarked.

12" tall   **$200-$250**
10" tall   **$100-$125**

Three 9" matte white vases, from left: two-handled vase, 1930s, McCoy mark; large Swan vase, 1950s (generally, colored glazes were earlier, mid-1940s); Sailboat vase (seen here with round bottom, sailboat motif also found on narrower vase with square bottom). **$70-$90 each**

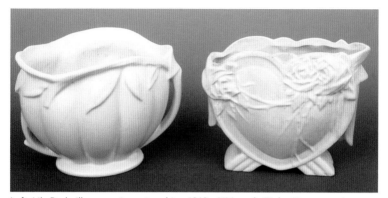

Left: Lily Bud pillow vase in matte white, 1940s, NM mark. Right: Heart vase in matte white, 1940s, unmarked, each 6" tall. **$60-$70 each**

Sand Dollar vase in matte white, stoneware, 1940s, unmarked, also found in pastel colors, and brown and green. **$250-$300,** depending on color

Butterfly cylinder vase with under-glaze decoration, 1940s, NM mark, 8" tall. **$350-$450** (in typical colors of coral, yellow, blue, or green, **$60-$90**)

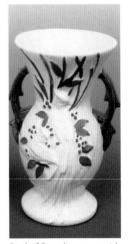

Two Drape-handle vases in matte white, 1940s, unmarked, also found in 6", 8", and 10" sizes, and glossy
green, blue, and yellow. 12" tall $90-$110
9" tall $60-$75

Bird of Paradise vase with
cold paint decoration
(not factory), found in
glossy colors, late 1940s,
unmarked, 8 1/4" tall.
$40-$50

Two Magnolia vases, left example having the more typical glaze combination, early
1950s, McCoy mark, 8 1/2" tall. $250-$300 each

Hyacinth vases in a range of glazes, early 1950s, McCoy mark, 8" tall. **$150-$225 each,** depending on glaze intensity and mold crispness

Tall Double Tulip vases in a range of glazes, late 1940s, McCoy mark, 8" tall.
$100-$125 each

Low Double Tulip vases, with right example having the more typical glaze, early 1950s, McCoy mark, 6 1/2" tall. **$225-$250 each**

Two Poppy vases in pink and yellow (harder to find), mid-1950s, McCoy mark.
$800-$1,000 each, depending on glaze intensity and mold crispness

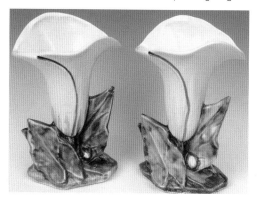

Single Lily bud vases, usually white or yellow with decoration under glaze, late 1940s, McCoy mark, 8" tall. **$90-$110 each**

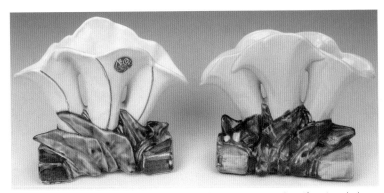

Triple Lily vases, one with original paper label, seen in matte white (front) and glossy yellow (back), also comes in glossy white, early 1950s, McCoy mark, 8 1/2" tall.
$100-$125 each

Two Wild Rose vases with atypical glaze combinations, usually blue, lavender, pink, and yellow (with pink flowers), early 1950s, McCoy mark.
In these colors
$175-$200 each
In common colors
$80-$100 each

Two Chrysanthemum vases in typical glazes, early 1950s, McCoy mark, 8 1/4" tall.
$150-$200 each,
depending on glaze intensity and mold crispness

Two Chrysanthemum vases in atypical glazes, early 1950s, McCoy mark 8 1/4" tall.
Left   **$150-$200**
Right   **$275-$300**

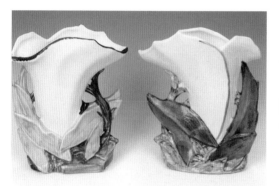

Two Large Lily vases in typical glazes (blue leaves are matte, green are glossy), mid-1950s, McCoy mark, 8 1/2" tall.
$500-$600 each

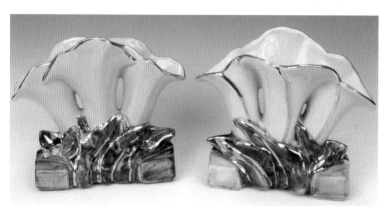

Triple Lily vases with gold trim, early 1950s, McCoy mark, 8 1/2" tall. **$125-$150 each**

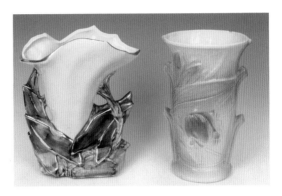

Left: large Lily vase in gold trim, mid-1950s, McCoy mark, 8 1/2" tall. **$700-$800**
Right: rare Tulip vase in air-brush decoration, 1950s, McCoy mark, 8 1/4" tall.
$800-$1,000

Left: Low Double Tulip vase in gold trim, early 1950s, McCoy USA mark, 6 1/2" tall.
$325-$375
Right: Magnolia vase in gold trim, early 1950s, McCoy mark, 8 1/2" tall. **$350-$400**

Three Leaves and Berries fan vases, commonly found in aqua, pink, white and yellow; cobalt blue is hard to find, and the under-glaze decorated example at left is very rare; late 1930s or early 40s, McCoy USA or unmarked, 6" tall. Left   **$175-$200**
Center   **$110-$125**
Right   **$75-$90**
(Beware of reproductions, which are lighter, have soft mold details, and thinner glazes.)

Two Leaves and Berries fan vases in white and burgundy, 1940s, burgundy with round McCoy USA mark, white with McCoy USA mark, 6" tall.
$70-$90 each

Ring ware vase, 1920s, unmarked, 9 1/4" tall. **$100-$125**

Vase once thought to be Shawnee but later found in a McCoy catalog page, late 1940s, unmarked, 6 1/2" tall.
$35-$45

Left: Double Bud vase in glossy green, 1940s, Mc-Coy or unmarked, also found in aqua, cobalt blue, turquoise, and yellow, 8" tall. **$75-$90**
Right: Stepped-Base vase in glossy green, 1940s, round McCoy USA mark, 7" tall. **$40-$45**

Two Hourglass vases, Stoneware, 1930s, un-marked, 5" tall (a hard-to-find size). **$70-$90 each**

Left: "V" vase in glossy green glaze, mid-1920s, V2 mark, this style also found without handles, 9" tall. **$90-$110**
Right: "Number 50" vase in glossy burgundy, 1930s, unmarked, 9" tall.
$100-$125

Three vases in blue. Left: Double Bud vase in glossy cobalt, 1940s, NM mark, also found in aqua, dark green, turquoise, and yellow. **$75-$90**
Center: Stoneware vase in blue with "flat flower," 1930s, unmarked, 7" tall. **$175-$200**
Right: Two-handled vase in cobalt, 1950s, unmarked, 7" tall. **$40-$50**

Ivy vase (also called English Ivy) in an atypical maroon and yellow, hand-painted, (normally white or yellow), 1950s, McCoy mark, 9" tall.
As shown **$800+**
Normally **$125-$150**

Vase with low drape handles in glossy blue glaze, 1940s, unmarked, 10" tall.
$80-$90

Two Leaves and Berries vases (sometimes called the stovepipe), 1930s, unmarked, in what McCoy called "onyx" glazes, 8" tall. **$80-$90 each**

Left: Two-handled vase with post-factory decoration, 1940s, NM mark (reproductions found with McCoy mark), 9" tall. **$40-$45**
Right: Lizard handle vase in matte white with post-factory decoration, mid- to late-1930s, unmarked, 9" tall (also comes in 10"). **$200-$225** (also found in green and brown)

Left: Blossomtime vase in atypical glaze (white flower), mid-1940s, McCoy mark, 8" tall. **$100-$150**
Right: Non-production vase with applied berries and leaves, hand cut from a taller vase, ex-Cope Collection, 5" tall. **No established value.**

Leaves and Berries urn-form vase in matte white with small handles and unusual interior ring pattern, hard to find form, stoneware, 1930s, 8" tall.
$300-$350

Non-production vase in a variation on the Blossomtime form, with applied flowers and decorated under glaze, mid-1940s, 8" tall. **No established value.**

Tall Fan vase in atypical glossy white (normally found in chartreuse and green, or yellow and maroon), mid-1950s, McCoy mark, 15" tall, also found in 10".
As shown   **$350-$400**
Same size, other colors   **$150-$200**
10" size   **$75-$90**

Poppy vase in gold trim, 1950s, McCoy mark, reverse not gold trimmed, 8 1/2" wide.   **$1,000-$1,200**

Large Swan vase and two-handled vase, both in gold trim, 1950s to 1960s, Mc-Coy USA, 9" tall.
$90-$100 each

Fawn vase and Chicken pitcher vase (also with floral decal) in gold trim, 1950s, McCoy and McCoy USA mark.
Fawn vase, 9" tall
$125-$150
Chicken **$90-$110**

Two vases in glossy yellow and pink with gold trim, 1950s, Mc-Coy USA and Shafer marks, also found in blue and white, 9" tall. **$90-$110 each**

Two vases in gold trim. Left: Ivy motif (also called English Ivy), 1950s, McCoy USA mark, 9" tall. **$150-$175** Right: Tulip motif, 1950s, USA mark, also with hand-applied inscription, "M.W. Rosendahl, 1955," 8" tall. **$100-$125**

Left: Low Double Tulip vase in gold trim, early 1950s, McCoy USA mark, 6 1/2" tall. Right: Triple Lily vase with gold trim, early 1950s, McCoy mark, 8 1/2" tall. **$175-$225**

Two gold trim vases. Left: Magnolia, 1950s, McCoy USA mark, 7 1/2" tall. **$250-$300** Right: Hyacinth, 1950s, McCoy USA mark, slightly duller gold finish, probably by McCoy, not Shafer, 8" tall. **$400-$425**

Two presentation vases in gold trim. Left: Tulip motif, 1950s, McCoy mark, also with hand-applied inscription, "50 Golden Years" and signed E.P. Aurand, 8" tall. Right: McCoy mark, with hand-applied inscription, "1949 Iowa State Glad Show, Waterloo," signed E.P.A., 9" tall.
$125-$150 each

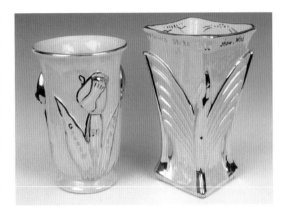

Two gold trim vases. Left: Sunflower, 1950s, unmarked, 9" tall. Right: Ewer with hand-painted grapes under glaze, late 1940s, initialed W, 9" tall.
$150-$175 each

Two gold trim vases. Left: Bird and Berries, 1950s, McCoy USA mark, 8" tall.
$125-$150
Right: Petal vase (also called Celery vase), 1950s, McCoy USA mark, 9" tall.
$250-$300

Two Ripple Ware vases in gold trim, glossy yellow and turquoise, early 1950s, McCoy mark, also found in other colors with dripping glazed rims, 7" tall.
$90-$110 each

Left: Grape vase in gold trim, 1950s, McCoy USA mark, also found with brown and green glazes, 9" tall.
$90-$110
Right: Sunburst gold vase, 1950s, faint McCoy USA mark, 6" tall. **$60-$75**

Three miniature flower holders in Sunburst gold (the Cornucopia and Swan are "ladder pieces," so named because they were pictured in a early McCoy guide on a drying rack that was tiered like the steps of a ladder), 1940s to 1950s, unmarked, 3 1/4" tall. **$60-$70**, depending on color

Phial vase in dusty pink, mid-1980s, Designer Accents with USA and 44 mark, 12" wide.   **$25-$30**

Large Fan vase, also called "Blades of Grass," glossy black, late 1950s, McCoy USA mark, 10" tall.   **$175-$225**

Non-production vase with carved leaves and branches, 1948, McCoy Made in USA mark with initials "TK," ex-Ty Kuhn collection, 8" tall. **No established value.**

Tall Scroll vase in matte green (often found in glossy tan-brown), late 1940s, USA mark, 14" tall. **$150-$200**

Hand vase with separated fingers and painted nails, 1950s, NM USA mark, 6 1/2" tall.   **$125-$150**

Five Swan flower holders in matte colors (called "ladder pieces," so named because they were pictured in a early McCoy guide on a drying rack that was tiered like the steps of a ladder), 1940s, NM USA mark, 3 1/4" tall. Usually **$60-$70**, but yellow and pink (the only one found in glossy finish) may bring **$100-$125**.

Two Disc vases in glossy cobalt blue and burgundy, 1940s, also found in yellow and white, USA mark, 6 3/4" tall.
$100-$125 each

Five Pitcher flower holders, 1940s, NM USA mark, 3 1/4" tall. In pink blue and yellow. **$80-$90 each** In coral and hand-painted **$150-$200 each**

Three Pigeon or Dove flower holders (called "ladder pieces," so named because they were pictured in a early McCoy guide on a drying rack that was tiered like the steps of a ladder), 1940s, USA mark, 3 1/2" tall, 1940s. **$100-$125 each**

Six Praying Hands flower holders, 1940s, NM USA mark, 3" tall, **$100-$125 each** except for white and aqua, **$50-$60**

Six miniature Cornucopia flower holder in matte colors, 1940s, NM USA mark, 3 1/4" tall. Blue, white, aqua **$50-$60**
Pink and yellow **$125-$150**
Coral **$175-$225**

Five Turtle flower holders (also called miniature planters), 1940s, NM USA mark, 4 1/4" long. Aqua and white **$40-$50**
Blue **$70-$80**
Pink and yellow **$125-$150 each**

Four 5" Basket-weave vases in glossy burgundy, green, white, and blue **$40-$50 each**

Two vases in matte aqua, 1940s, un-marked or USA mark, 9" tall.
$50-$60 each

Two vases in matte yellow and aqua, 1940s, NM USA mark, also found in white, 8" tall. **$50-$60 each**

Two vases with leaves and stylized flow-ers in glossy green and matte aqua, stoneware, late 1920s, unmarked, 7" tall.
$110-$125 each

Two Basket-weave vases in glossy aqua and green, 6" and 7". **$45-$55 each**

Left: Hobnail and Leaves vase in glossy aqua, 1940s, NM USA mark, 7" tall.
$75-$85
Right: Ring ware vase with handles in glossy green, 1940s, McCoy USA mark, 5 1/2" tall. **$50-$60**

Left: Vase in glossy aqua with hand-painted flowers, 1940s, McCoy mark, 8" tall. **$125-$150** because of painting; normally **$60-$70**
Right: Cornucopia vase in glossy aqua, 1940s, round McCoy mark, 7" tall.
$50-$60

Left: Fluted vase with zigzag top in glossy aqua, 1950s, McCoy USA mark, 10" tall (also found in 8 and 14" sizes). **$90-$110**
Right: Vase in glossy aqua, 1940s, unmarked or NM mark, 8" tall. **$50-$60**

Two vases in glossy aqua. Left: 1940s, round McCoy mark, 9" tall. **$45-$55**
Right: Square Cherry vase, stoneware, 1930s, round McCoy mark, 12" tall. **$125-$150**

Left: Two-handled vase in glossy aqua, 1940s, McCoy mark. **$50-$60**
Right: Uncle Sam vase in glossy aqua, 1940s, incised McCoy mark, 7 1/2" tall, also found in yellow and white. **$60-$70**
(Beware of reproductions, which may be slightly smaller.)

Three vases in glossy aqua. Left: 8" tall, round McCoy USA mark. **$25-$35**
Center: 12" tall, McCoy USA mark, also found in yellow and white. **$50-$60**
Right: 7 1/2" tall, round McCoy USA mark, found in other colors. **$25-$35**

Vase with fired-on decoration, art nouveau influence similar to Brush-McCoy, 1920s, unmarked, 8" tall. **$450-$500**

Two Deer and Cornucopia vases, 1950s, McCoy USA mark, 9" tall, right example in rare brown and green.
Left   **$70-$80**
Right   **$125-$150**

Pitcher vase, 1950s, McCoy USA mark, 7 1/2" tall.
$25-$35

Two vases, one with fired-on decoration (possibly a lunch-hour piece), 1940s, USA mark, 10" tall.
With decoration   **$125-$150**
Without   **$75-$90**

Left: Sailboat vase with square bottom in matte aqua, 1940s, NM USA or NM mark, other matte colors, 9" tall. **$85-$95**
Right: Two-handled vase in matte aqua, 1940s, McCoy mark, other matte colors, 9" tall. **$55-$65**

Two matte aqua vases, 10" tall, found in
other matte colors.
Left: Unmarked $85-$95
Right: Arrow leaf, McCoy mark $125-$150

Two matte aqua vases, 9" tall. Left:
1940s, McCoy mark, found in both matte
and glossy colors. $55-$65
Right: Urn vase, 1940s, USA mark, rarely
found in other matte colors. $75-$85

Two matte aqua vases, 10" and 11 1/2" tall.
Left: 1940s, USA mark $75-$85
Right: 1930s, unmarked, Stoneware
                                $150-$175
Also found in sizes ranging from
6" to 18".

Two matte aqua vases, 12" tall. Left:
1940s, NM mark, frequently found with
spots of other glazes, commonly cobalt
blue. $150-$175
Right: Strap vase, usually found in glossy
colors. $175-$225

Left: Hobnail "V" vase
in matte lavender,
1940s, NM USA mark,
9" tall. $110-$125
Center and right: Two
Hobnail vases in matte
aqua, 6" and 8", 1940s,
NM USA mark.
6" tall $55-$65
8" tall $90-$110

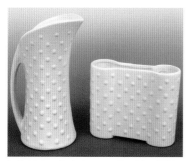

Left: Hobnail pitcher vase in white, 1940s, NM USA Mark, 10" tall. **$125-$150**
Right: Hobnail castle gate or "binoculars" vase in white, 1940s, unmarked, 6" tall. **$175-$200**

Two matte aqua floor vases, 14" tall.
Left: rib or fin vase, 1930s, unmarked, matte colors or drip glazes. **$500+**
Right: Sand Dollar vase, 1930s and '40s, unmarked, matte or glossy colors. **$250-$300**

Two matte aqua vases, 8 1/2" and 10"
Left: 1940s, round McCoy USA mark, found in matte and glossy colors. **$65-$75**
Right: 1940s, McCoy mark, other matte colors. **$65-$75**

Two matte aqua vases, 8" and 7". Left: Tulip vase, 1940s, USA mark, matte and glossy colors. **$75-$85**
Right: Leafy vase, found in matte colors, 1940s, unmarked. **$150-$175**

Two matte aqua vases, 9" and 7" Left: Swan vase, 1940s, McCoy mark. **$55-$65**
Right: Cornucopia vase, 1940s, McCoy mark. **$45-$55**

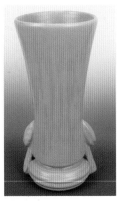

Floor vase in matte aqua, stoneware, 1930s or '40s, unmarked, matte and glossy colors, 18" tall (rare this size). **$1,200+**

Two Butterfly Line vases. Left: Matte blue pitcher, 1940s, NM USA mark, 10" tall. **$175-$200**
Right: Cylinder vase in matte aqua, 1940s, NM USA mark, 6" tall. **$55-$65**

Two Butterfly Line Castle Gate or "Binoculars" vases, 1940s, USA mark or unmarked, found in other matte colors, 6" tall.
$185-$215 each

Left: Two-handled vase in matte aqua, 1940s, unmarked, 6 1/2" tall.
$55-$65
Right: Vase in glossy yellow (also found in burgundy and blue), 1940s, round McCoy mark, 8" tall.
$60-$70

Two Phial vases in lavender and blue, mid-1980s, Designer Accents, marked 458 and USA, 12" tall.
$45-$50 each

Scandia Line floor vase, 1970s, McCoy LCC mark, 14 1/2" tall.* **$45-$55**

Garden Club vase in matte yellow, late 1950s, McCoy USA mark, 9 1/2" tall.
$150-$175

Pitcher vase, 1970s (later version of a 1940s piece), USA mark or unmarked 5" tall. **$25-$35**

Vase (collectors call this the "Shrimp vase" because of its common coloration) with applied maple leaves in atypical blue-black and yellow glaze (usually in chartreuse or salmon with green leaves), 1950s, McCoy USA mark, 9" tall.
As shown   **$600+**
In common colors   **$175-$225**

Lily Bud pillow vase in matte aqua, 1940s, NM USA mark, 6 1/2" tall. **$75-$85**

Arcature vase in atypical dark lavender glaze (usually green and yellow), early 1950s, McCoy USA mark, 6 3/4" tall.
In normal colors **$50-$60**
As shown **$150-$200**

Pine cone vase, not a production piece, mid-1940s, McCoy USA mark, 9 1/2" tall. **$800-$1,000**

Left: Rope-handle pitcher vase in matte aqua, late 1930s, unmarked, 7" tall. **$55-$65**
Right: Cornucopia vase in matte aqua, 1940s, unmarked, 5 1/2" tall. **$55-$65**

A grouping of what collectors call the "5" vases" (though actual sizes vary by up to half an inch). Many vase styles are hard to find this size, and so this has become an entire collecting category. They are unmarked. Prices vary from about **$60** to more than **$125** depending on style, glaze, and mold quality, and how badly a collector needs one to complete a set.

Classic Line bud vases, early 1960s, Mc-Coy USA mark, 8" tall. **$35-$45 each**

Grecian urn vase, 9 1/2" tall, 1950s. **$110-$125**

Ring ware vase in glossy burgundy, 1920s, unmarked, 9 1/4" tall. **$100-$125**

Lily Bud pillow vase in glossy rose/pink, 1940s, NM USA mark, 7" tall. **$90-$110**

Three Leaves and Berries vases with tab or ear handles in matte white, 1930s, unmarked.
5" tall   **$80-$90**
8" tall   **$90-$110**

Ribbed vase in atypical brown glaze, 1940s, unmarked, 6 1/2" tall. **$55-$65**

Sunflower vase using same mold as lamp, 1950s, with unusual air-brush decoration, unmarked. **$450-$550**

Wall Pockets

Wall pockets by nature are easily damaged, so collectors should look for signs of restoration around chipped holes and on high points, and paint touch-ups on those made with cold-paint decoration. Examples in gold trim command a higher price.

Apple wall pocket in gold trim, 1950s, unmarked, 7" long. **$200-$225**

Bananas wall pocket, green leaves, with gold trim, 1950s, unmarked, 7" long. **$400-$450**

Basket-weave Horn of Plenty wall pocket, 1950s, McCoy USA mark, 8" long. **$100-$120**

Blossomtime wall pocket in matte yellow, McCoy mark, 7 3/4" long. **$90-$110**

Butterfly wall pocket in matte aqua with crisp mold, 1940s, NM mark, 6" tall.
$450-$550

Fan wall pocket in gold Brocade, found in other colors and gold trimmed, 1950s, McCoy USA and 24 kt. gold marks, 8 1/2" wide.
$85-$95

Clown or Jester wall pocket with cold-paint decoration, 1940s, Mc-Coy mark, 8 1/2" long.
$90-$110
(depending on paint condition)

Cuckoo Clock wall pocket in gold trim (comes with both Roman and Arabic numerals, and in a range of colors), 1950s, Mc-Coy mark, 8" tall without weights. **$200-$225**

Blossomtime wall pocket in matte white, McCoy mark, 7 3/4" long.
$90-$110

Three Flower form wall pockets, late 1940s, unmarked, 6" tall.
Blue and coral, common colors **$40-$50**
Center, with under-glaze decoration **$175-$225**

Grapes wall pocket in gold trim, 1950s, unmarked, 7" long. **$300-$350**

Iron on a Trivet wall pocket, 1950s, McCoy USA, 8" long. **$85-$95**

Lily wall pocket in yellow, McCoy mark, 6 1/2" long. **$80-$100**

Fancy Lily Bud wall pocket in matte aqua, 1940s, incised McCoy mark, 8" long.
$225-$250

Large Lily Bud wall pocket in matte aqua, 1940s, NM USA mark, 8" long.
$150-$175

Small Lily Bud wall pocket in matte aqua, 1940s, NM USA mark, 6" long. **$65-$75**

Lady in the Bonnet wall pocket with cold-paint decoration, 1940s, McCoy mark, wide variety of paint colors and details, 8" long. **$70-$80**

Lovebirds on a Trivet wall pocket, 1950s, McCoy USA mark, 8" long. **$75-$85**

Mexican Man wall pocket in matte aqua, 1940s, NM USA mark, 7 1/2" long. **$65-$75**

Mailbox wall pocket, early 1950s, McCoy USA mark, also found with cold-paint decoration. **$90-$110** (beware of reproductions in bright pastels)

Owls on a Trivet wall pocket with some cold-paint decoration, 1950s, McCoy USA mark, 8" long. **$75-$85**

Umbrella wall pocket, 1950s, McCoy USA mark, found in other colors including gold Brocade Line, 8 1/4" long. **$75-$85**

Violin wall pocket in black, a hard to find color. **$350-$400**

Violin wall pocket in blue with gold trim, 1950s, McCoy USA and Shafer mark, 10" long. **$275-$325**

Urn wall pocket in speckled pink glaze with gold trim, McCoy USA mark, also found in chartreuse, 4 1/2" long. **$75-$85**

Pear wall pocket in gold trim, 1950s, unmarked, 7" long. **$200-$225**

A collection of Fruit wall pockets, and the corresponding fruit planters.

Miscellaneous

This section includes ashtrays, bookends, console bowls, boxes, ornaments, and other accessories, and some rare non-production pieces.

There was no shortage of selections available in mugs from McCoy in a 1977 catalog.

(A) 144G, 144S
HOLLY LEAF (with votive drop-in)
2¾" x 5¾" dark green w/red
berries, pk. 12, wt. 10 lbs.
2.50

(B) 146G, 146S
HOLLY PEDESTAL (uses large
red pillar candle)
pk. 24, wt. 12 lbs.
$2.50

(C) 141W
CROSS (small)
cut out for use with votive,
10½" x 6½", pk. 6, 10 lbs.
$6.00

*(D) 138W, 138S
SANTA (holes star-shaped for use
with votive)
white glaze or sandstone,
6" x 4", pk. 12, wt. 12 lbs.
Glaze-$4.00, Sandstone-$3.50.

*(E) 139CTW, 139CTS
MRS. SANTA (candle top)
white glaze or sandstone,
5¾" x 3½", pk. 12, wt. 12 lbs.
Glaze-$4.00, Sandstone-$3.50.

(F) 140M
LARGE SNOWMAN (decorated)
7" x 5", pk. 6, wt. 9 lbs.
$5.00

*(G) 139W, 139S
MRS. SANTA (holes star-shaped
for use with votive)
white glaze or sandstone,
5¾" x 3½" pk. 12, wt. 12 lbs.
Glaze-$4.00, Sandstone-$3.50.

(H) M137G, M137W, M137S
CHRISTMAS TREE (large)
9½" x 9" Green or white tipped
w/green, pk. 6, wt. 20 lbs.
7.95

*(I) 138CTW, 138CTS
SANTA (candle top)
white glaze or sandstone,
6" x 4", pk. 12, wt. 12 lbs.
Glaze-$4.00, Sandstone-$3.50.

McCoy Limited advertised "Christmas Scarf People" and ceramic Christmas trees as part of its holiday line.

Republican ashtray in gold trim, 1960s, inscribed on bottom, "Designed by Paul Genter," also found in other colors with raised outline of Ohio, 6" diameter. **$45-$50**

Lily bookends, 1940s, McCoy Made in USA mark, 6" tall.
$125-$150/pair

Flower form bookends/planters, 1950s, McCoy USA mark, also found in green and yellow, cream and green, 6" tall.
$150-$175/pair

Lily bookends with pearly glaze in gold trim, 1940s to '50s, sometimes marked McCoy USA, usually unmarked, 5 1/2" tall. **$225-$275/pair**

Lily Bud bookends in matte aqua, 1940s, NM USA mark, 5 3/4" tall. **$200-$250/pair**

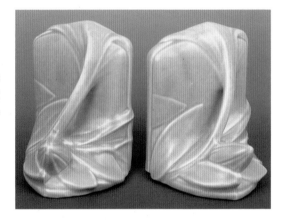

Parakeets (also called lovebirds) bookends in matte aqua, early 1940s, NM mark. **$200-$250/pair**

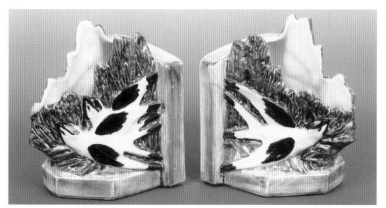

Swallow bookends/planter, 1950s, McCoy USA mark, 6" tall. **$275-$325/pair**

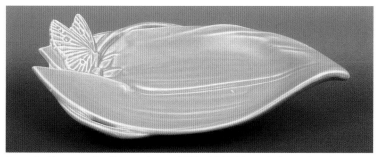

Butterfly Line console dish or platter, 1940s, NM USA mark, found in other matte colors, 14" long. **$350-$400**

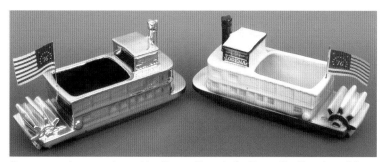

Commemorative steamboats (the "Lorena") made for Zanesville Chamber of Commerce, 1976, 7" long. **$70-$80**

Left: Nelson and Billie McCoy retirement mug, 1981.　　**$100-$125**
Right: Nelson McCoy Pottery Co. mug.　　**$80-$90**

Two Butterfly Line pin dishes (also called console bowls) in matte blue and yellow, 1940s, NM USA mark, 5" diameter.　　**$55-$65 each**

Pickling crock and butter churn, with original tag and dasher, Lancaster Colony, 1980s, 12 1/2" tall.

$60-$70 each

Lily Bud console bowls in 5 1/2" and 11 1/2" widths, 1940s, NM mark. 5 1/2" **$40-$50**
11 1/2"　　**$125-$150**
Two Lily Bud candleholders in matte aqua, 1940s, NM mark, 5 1/2" diameter.

$75-$85/pair

Lily Bud 8 1/2" console bowl in matte lavender. **$65-$75**

All three sizes of Lily Bud console bowls, including 8 1/2" size. **$65-$75**

Console bowl with candleholders, stoneware, late 1930s, more common in green, bowl, 8" diameter. **$350-$450/set**
Green **$200/set**

Cuspidor with grapes motif in glossy brown, 1940s, unmarked, 7 1/2" diameter. **$50-$60**

Three-section Leaf candy or snack dish, early 1950s, McCoy mark, 11" wide, also found in Rustic glazes of green and brown.
As shown **$100-$125**
Rustic **$50-$60**

Leaf dish, ex-Cope Collection, unmarked 12" long. **$1,200+**

Cupid Pig pitcher (model for smaller commemorative issued by McCoy Collection), only the second in this size known to exist, with damage, 9" tall.
$500-$700

Fawn flower bowl ornament (one of the "ladder pieces," so named because they were pictured in an early McCoy guide on a drying rack that was tiered like the steps of a ladder), 1940s to 1950s, usually found in white or brown glaze, this one is ex-Ty Kuhn collection and painted by Kuhn.

As shown **$175-$200**
Normally **$90-$110**

Left: Trinket box in atypical glaze, 1970s, McCoy USA mark, ex-Ty Kuhn collection. **$90-$110**
Below: Glaze screen, cast iron with mesh, used to screen glaze compounds, and trimming knife used to clean unfired pottery after removal from molds.
Knife **$125**
Screen **$200**

Miniature teapot with hand-painted decoration under glaze on raised grape design, this variation was never produced, but a similar pot with flat decoration was made, 3 1/2" tall. **$300-$350**
Ceramic plaque designed for use as a pin, but without pin back, ex-Cope Collection. Not a product of McCoy.

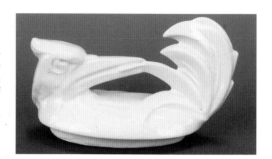

Lid from a covered casserole in the form of a long-billed bird with crest, lid also found in glossy brown but without crest. **No established value.**

Double Giraffe vase, not produced, a green and tan example is in the Cope Gallery in Roseville, Ohio; McCoy mark, 9 1/2" tall. **$5,000**

Double candleholder, 1930s (?), raised McCoy mark but not a production piece, 9 1/2" tall, only two others known to exist in the Cope Gallery. **$3,000-$5,000**

Double Angelfish and Seahorses flower bowl ornaments or aquarium decorations, 1940s, unmarked, 6" and 6 1/4" tall, also found in green.

Fish $200-$250
Seahorses $300-$350

Fish flower bowl ornament (one of a kind?), 1950s, USA mark, 4 1/2" tall. **$2,300+**

Two key minders, 1960s. **$50-$75 each**

Four flower bowl ornaments (the witch, gnome, and pelican are "ladder pieces," so named because they were pictured in an early McCoy guide on a drying rack that was tiered like the steps of a ladder), 1940s to 1950s, usually found in white or brown (rare) glaze, USA or unmarked, about 3" tall.

Cat and witch **$400-$450**
Gnome **$300-$325**
Pelican **$400-$425**

Three flower bowl ornaments or flower holders (fish), 1940s to 1950s, usually found in white, yellow, green, or brown glaze, USA or unmarked.

Fish, 3" tall **$150-$200**
Rabbit, 1 1/2" tall **$300-$350**

Foreground: Console bowl with applied grapes in gold trim, 1950s, McCoy USA and Shafer marks and an employee stamp "Z," 12" long.   **$60-$75**
Gondola candy dish in gold trim, this example has the oar support, which is missing on some dishes, 1950s, McCoy mark, 11 1/2" long.
$60-$75

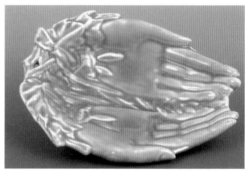

Large Hands novelty dish in glossy aqua, 1940s, NM USA mark, 8 1/2" long.
$125-$150

Hands novelty dish (sometimes called an ashtray) in gold trim, 1940s, NM USA mark, 5 3/4" long.
$70-$80

Five flower bowl ornaments in matte white (the first four from left are "ladder pieces," so named because they were pictured in an early McCoy guide on a drying rack that was tiered like the steps of a ladder), 1940s, usually found in white or brown (rare) glaze, unmarked, from 3 3/4" to 4 3/4" tall.　　　　　**$100-$125 each**

GOP convention commemorative (1956?), unmarked, 5 1/2" tall.　　　　**$90-$110**

Ashtray, a lunch-hour piece, with applied heart and the words "MA" and "PA," marked McCoy on reverse, made from the bottom of a Cornucopia vase, 6 1/2" by 3 1/4". **$200-$300**

Christmas items: left, covered jar dated 1973, 5 3/4" tall; right, coffee mug dated 1967 and marked "The Kuhns," 5" tall. **$30-$40 each**

Two Brocade pieces: round covered dish and trinket box, possibly part of a dresser set, 1950s, McCoy USA 464 mark. **$80-$90/pair**

Two Cowboy Boot pencil holders, 1973, normally brown, these are in test glazes with formula notes by Ty Kuhn, 5" tall.

$100 each

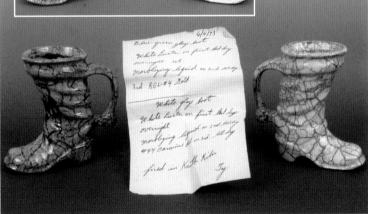

Bull dresser caddie made for Swank, 1960s, unmarked, 10" long. **$25-$35**

Lion dresser caddie made for Swank, 1960s, unmarked, 10" long. **$55-$65**

Racehorse dresser caddie made for Swank with clothes brush tail, 1960s, unmarked, 9" long not including tail.

$75-$85

Dog dresser caddie made for Swank with shoehorn tail, 1960s, unmarked, 11" long. **$45-$55**

1932 Pierce Arrow decanter made for Jim Beam, 1960s, McCoy mark, 11" long.

$75-$85

Lion statue, 1960s, unmarked, 15" long. **$45-$55**

Left: Hung-over dog bank made for Swank, 1960s, unmarked, 6" tall; right: Eagle bank, 1960s, unmarked, 7" tall. **$50-$60 each**

Two Grecian Line console bowls (8" and 12" diameter, McCoy USA mark, number 444) and candleholders (4" diameter, unmarked), 1950s.

12" bowl	**$80-$90**
8" bowl	**$50-$60**
Candleholders	**$90-$110/pair**

DISCARP

Fake and Confusing Marks on McCoy Pottery

By Mark Chervenka

A new frog sprinkler marked McCoy USA. The frog is a direct copy of a McCoy original, but the original McCoy piece was made as a planter only, never as a sprinkler with a handle.

The raised molded "McCoy USA" mark on the bottom of the new frog sprinkler.

Historically, collectors have relied on marks to authenticate and date antiques and collectibles. That process is becoming less reliable as more reproductions are appearing with nearly exact copies of original marks.

Some old company names have been legitimately reregistered in America, but most marks on reproductions are deliberately designed to be confusing. In many cases, very slight variations—such as color, whether a mark is raised or impressed, whether the mark includes the country of origin—are all that separate vintage marks from the fakes.

Fake and confusing marks have become so widespread that marks alone should never be used as a single test of age or authenticity. Examine a variety of features on a piece including shape, colors, pattern, and decoration before making a conclusion on age. Perhaps the best defense against fake marks is simply a healthy skepticism.

New pottery McCoy is one of the most common reproductions in today's market. The new McCoy marks are virtually identical to marks on originals. The marks appear on copies of specific McCoy originals as well as fantasy items never made by McCoy.

Reproductions that copy original McCoy shapes are the most difficult to identify. Since molds used to make the reproductions are taken from authentic samples, new and old shapes are almost impossible to separate. Questionable pieces should be carefully measured and compared to originals in reference books. The reproductions are one-quarter to three-quarters of an inch smaller than the originals.

This wall vase/planter marked McCoy is a fantasy piece: No original was ever made by McCoy. A piece from another manufacturer was used to make a mold, and a fake McCoy mark was added.